Ahali

An anthology for sett

BEDFORD PRESS

Table of Contents

Ahali

an anthology for setting a setting

Can Altay

Continued from the cover

The issues of *Ahali: a journal for setting a setting* have been treated as hovering frame structures, offering a number of entry points to each contribution. From the first invitation, the journal has always been open to a diverse set of works including project descriptions, existing texts (published or unpublished), outlines of sketches and ideas, proposals, theme-specific writing or interviews. The works, however, were never tied together by a theme; contributions could easily fall under one or many more 'issues'. A similar spirit applies to the contributions in this anthology, but for the sake of a more structured reading, I have tried to anchor some of those hovering frame structures to set a position and vantage point for individual contributions. In retrospect, these three chapters offer to provide a clear scope of interest for *Ahali*.

The journal's issues include topics such as: support, control and letting go; model-making for the socio-spatio-economic-political on propositions and implementation; cohabitation and parasitical practice; locatedness (and education); recycling, reconfiguration and sustainable excess; community and contingency; forecasting broken pasts; and becoming globe.

I prefer to see the contributions to *Ahali* as essays (regardless of differences in their form or attitude) because they try out ideas and offer reflections through their own particular means. All of the essays here have either deliberately or indirectly tapped into the issues of *Ahali* through the years, and those traces can easily be read in the three chapters that comprise this anthology. The first of these chapters is rooted in the name of the journal and the anthology itself: 'Ahali'. The 'C-Fact: Community, Collectivity, Constituency, Contingency' chapter questions what defines our modes of living together – as groups, as publics, as populations and also as the people of the earth. Each essay untangles varying degrees of togetherness and the responsibility that comes with it.

The second chapter, 'Model-Making: Propositions, Regulations, Patterns, Enthusiasms', investigates the dual-faceted process of models and their production. On the one hand, model-making can offer constructs to apply or imply at different scales; it therefore operates on an extraverted existence. On the other hand, model-making also refers to a kind of act, which requires intense focus and imagination that can only be found in enthusiasts, thus pointing to a very inward looking existence. I think it is this duality that brings together the seemingly different senses of the word 'model' and gives it power. The chapter follows this duality with a series of essays on the willingness or unwillingness to perform others' models while making one's own.

The third chapter of the *Ahali* anthology attempts to tackle our fleeting sense of time and history, and time's relationship to place. Essays in 'Forecasting Broken Pasts' try to reconcile or criticise such broken histories by offering ways we might imagine a future, or futures. Meanwhile, some of the essays here unite seemingly distinct pieces of time to critically construct affiliations, which then form constellations of events, places and realities.

I am grateful to all authors who have contributed to this anthology, and furthermore to every author who contributed to *Ahali*, the journal – they have trusted the project and supported it through their work. Asli Altay, who was Asli Kalinoglu when the project started, has constantly contributed to *Ahali* through her design input, which plays quite a significant role in the existence of both the journal and this anthology. I believe we also form a kind of *Ahali*, not only with select group of authors, but also with those involved in making the publication possible, the readers and the places where *Ahali* has appeared and will appear. Places have been particularly important to *Ahali* – from its first inception and launch in 2007 at Spike Island, Bristol; *Ahali* also appeared in Künstlerhaus Bethanien in Berlin; D21 in Leipzig; Künstlerhaus Stuttgart; Platform Garanti in Istanbul; Publish and Be Damned in London; Casco Office for Art, Design and Theory in Utrecht; now Bedford Press and the Architectural Association provide the grounds on which we may gather and disperse.

Transforming such a sporadic and growing collection of essays and artworks into an anthology was particularly hard. I made structured selections as the editor, for a publication, which, for five years, refused to be structured and sequenced. This anthology offers, perhaps, an asterism within a much larger constellation in order to give a sense of what issues relating to art, space and human existence myself and a group of fellow cultural producers have struggled with or been interested in. I certainly hope it makes sense and helps produce meaning when it comes to investigating issues of living together, model-making and coming to terms with recent pasts while imagining a future. In order to give due credit to all contributors of *Ahali* thus far, the full list of contributed essays are listed below.

1. Bik Van der Pol – Proposition for Reclaiming a Space
2. Binna Choi – Drawing Lesson (A Note)
3. Jason Coburn – adaptationStudy
4. Céline Condorelli – In Support
5. Claire Doherty – Curating Wrong Places...
6. Luca Frei – Untitled
7. James Hutchinson and Lesley Young – A Rational Anxiety
8. Jean-Christoph Lanquetin – Scénographies Urbaines
9. Jonathan Mosley & Sophie Warren – Point of Purchase
10. Jonathan Mosley & Sophie Warren – New Rogue Game
11. Ariane Müller – Sustainable Excess
12. Nils Norman – Museum
13. Paul O'Neill – Self-Organisation as a Way of Being
14. Paul O'Neill – Curating is the Answer, but What is the Question?
15. Emily Pethick and Annette Krauss – Hidden Curriculum
16. Public Works – Granville Cube
17. Jane Rendell – Letting Go
18. Robin Bone & Shep Steiner – We Field Workers
19. Robin Wilson – Opandshprop
20. Jeremiah Day – The Frank Church: River of No Return Wilderness
21. Markus Degerman – Hidden Agenda
22. Nav Haq – Ebony Tower: Strategy of the New Self-Othering

C-Fact

Community, Collectivity, Constituency, Contingency

We Field Workers

Robin Bone and Shep Steiner

Fall has arrived and a new term in the American Academy has begun; so to has a new flurry of visa problems: for foreign nationals living within the borders of the 'empire'. As Canadian citizens, we can work in the States under The North American Free Trade Agreement (NAFTA). The treaty and its extension, the Trade National (TN) Visa facilitates and serves the legitimate entrance requirements and purposes of a wide range of workers seeking employment in the United States. In secondary inspection from Tijuana to Sweetgrass, officers from Homeland Security are confronted by university professors and grape-pickers alike.

We 'field workers' from Canada and Mexico may enter the United States to work if we can produce a letter from our prospective employer, proper credentials, supporting documentation and a small processing fee of fifty dollars; $100 for Mexicans. The conditions for application and entrance are clear, but nothing ever goes as smoothly as predicted. The machine of state is calibrated to sputter and kick, and even on a government website, it is suggested that a lawyer who costs upwards of $1000 may be helpful. The term of one's stay is one calendar year.

I mention all of this because setting up life in the United States on a yearly basis has become a habit. We have tested out the possibilities of setting up a life in California, in Georgia, and finally in Florida. Our little traveling community of two – comprised of an art historian and physical therapist – prefers California. It feels more like home, but even putting down roots in the sunshine state can be difficult. Organic metaphors neither sprout nor proliferate inside machines. Things grow rather more fitfully in cracks, where odd pools form from leaky roofs, and in corners where a little light breaks through. The other thing that has become a habit of sorts is entering the country under duress;

experiencing first-hand the variable contingencies of the state and an unwieldy bureaucracy with changeable standards for admission; and finally, encountering an unpredictable mix of border guards whose temperaments range from the militant to that of the good Samaritan.

In any case, a pattern has developed. Thanks to a string of both unbending and helpful officers at a Montana port of entry, we have come to realise that it is an unwritten policy of the United States to refuse visas to field workers on the first attempt. Inasmuch, setting up community within the borders of Empire has of necessity to occur on the second attempt at entry. This does not mean a misinterpretation of the laws of state on the first bid is overcome for clarity, enlightenment and a correct interpretation of those laws on the second go-round. No, an event of another kind entirely has happened, a material event: call it reading according to the letter of the law, a moment of trauma proper, when the contingency of all community is recognised as such and settled in.

And so we often imagine a conversation taking place between migrant workers from Mexico and Canada. They are speaking across the wide chasm that is the United States. At first they are shouting, for each had been refused entry to the country that separates them, but having been granted entrance on their second attempt and now with each quite near the other, their voices become hushed. They are hopeful. It is only a narrow ditch which now divides them, and the day's work lies ahead of them. Fresh from their encounters with officers who have treated them both ill and well they talk of another place with great opportunity.

'It lies,' one says, 'beyond the borders of rightful entry and wrongful denial.'

'It is a field,' says the other. 'Let us meet there and together do our field work under the midday sun.'

Rogue Game

Jonathan Mosley and Sophie Warren with Can Altay

Event: Seek indoor sports hall with markings of at least three different overlaid
game courts or pitches.
    Enlist teams of players for each game.
    On court, assemble the players dressed to indicate team and game.
    On the whistle, let all games begin.
    Each game is played for its official duration.

Characteristics of the Rogue Game

playing amongst obstacles
advance and advantage
negotiation
collision
fracturing of order
stalling
stops, starts
fainting
indecision
clashes
game-swapping by players
interruption
rhythm, counter-rhythm,
synchronisation, syncopation
redundancy
non-accidentals
contra-action
contingent moves – liable but not certain to happen

Sophie Warren and Jonathan Mosley with Can Altay, Rogue Game at Spike Island, 2012. Photograph Max McClure.

Self-Organisation

As a way of being

Paul O'Neill

Beginning with a Personal Example

When I returned to Dublin in the late 1990s after living and working outside of Ireland, I realised that there were limited opportunities to show my work, curate exhibitions and engage the network of people I had established whilst away. As an artist, I faced a limited infrastructure in regards to working with other practitioners. I felt restricted in what I could do on a daily basis and in what I could offer as a host for potential moments of exchange with others.

In 1997, as an attempt to widen my existing network and create a space for these moments to happen, I founded MultiplesX with fellow artist Ronan McCrea. Initially, we meant for MultiplesX to serve as an intermediary solution for gallery space. After numerous formal and informal conversations concerning funding and exhibition space, Temple Bar Galleries (TBGS), with the support of the then-curator Vaari Claffey [1] and the design firm Language, became the central components in the organisational structure of our initiative. MultiplesX facilitated a space that supported a number of artists and curators over a short time span. Eventually it became a vehicle through which I could mobilise my thinking and speaking beyond the limitations of the subjective, and often isolationist, 'I' towards a more empowered position of the 'we'.

As a non-for-profit organisation we commissioned, organised and curated exhibitions of Irish and international artist's editions at regular intervals in the foyer at TBGS, and Language designed catalogues that distributed the works. We also organised touring exhibitions of works in Ireland, the UK and Europe, which extended our network of artists, curators and critics. A self-motivated initiative, MultiplesX began as a way of constructively addressing a lack of exhibition space, limited opportunities and a restrictive critical environment around what I as an artist, whose practice had shifted towards the curatorial, was interested in pursuing. Throughout the project I self-generated a network of curators, artists and practitioners with whom I have remained in contact and continue to collaborate on a regular basis. Rather than waiting for invitations from others to take part in projects, I was able to do the inviting myself with the knowledge that such relationships could facilitate further moments of exchange in the future. Establishing MultiplesX also enabled me to learn a wide range of administrative and organisational skills, such as applying for funding, handling artworks, writing press releases, consigning and insuring works, packing and transporting works, engaging other artists, gallerists, collectors, curators and critics and generally introducing a greater level of professionalism into my artistic and curatorial practice. And it was my earlier self-initiated projects of the 1990s that inspired me to consider MultiplesX as a possibility.

Although many MultiplesX objectives – such as establishing a market for emerging Irish art whilst finding galleries to represent established international artists not currently showing in Ireland – were either not met or badly timed, many of the skills, experiences and the network that emerged after MultiplesX informed my position when I entered my first institutional post as gallery curator at the London Print Studio between 2001–03. Since that time, I have been able to call upon the artists, curators and critics I met during my post, and I continue to work with and share an expanding cultural network among many of the participants. Like any self-initiated project, all physical and ephemeral voices have continued to provide new and unexpected perspectives. However, when considering methods of self-organisation, some projects become more expansive when they are more than the result of self-enterprise. By initiating and supporting the involvement of others in what one does, these projects can lead to a reflective, reciprocal kind of self-organisation.

Self-Initiated Projects: The First Stage of Self-Organisation

Self-initiated projects represented the first stage in configuring a world through which we wish to be read. By making connections between what we do and what others do, we can begin to enable pluralist forms of exchange. Initiators come from the position of wanting space of readership, as well as production, that is temporarily unavailable to them. There is recognition of an absence, which the initiator can make visible. By bringing this role into situations, individual positions can fall to the wayside, leaving room for and illuminating the connections between people.

As Mika Hannula has argued:

'Self-organisation is a so-called third space. It is a peculiar concentration of time and energy in a particular place where the interests of the participants in that context are debated, constituted, defined, clarified and defended. It does not belong to either A or B, but is constructed spontaneously through the interaction between A and B. It is a meeting point at which both sides have found the capacity to listen to each other on the other's terms. It is based on acknowledging interaction that seeks to negotiate a sustainable compromise for existing alongside one another, not as a unity, but in a plurality' [2].

Self-initiated projects are the life-blood of culture - ie culture as understood in both material production and as a symbolic system of that production [3]. Self-organisation is about making things happen on one's own terms alongside like-minded positions. Artists, curators or writers who initiate projects with others can self-direct notions of both 'commonality' and 'connectivity' in relation to how the involved want to position what they do and how it exists in the world. These two central terms function as inherent qualities within one's work: 'common' relates to the general idea of practice as a form of self-positioning alongside other like-minded positions while 'connected' conveys a belief that these other like-forms of practice can take part in the same critical discourse.

As Anthony Davies, Stephan Dillemuth and Jakob Jakobsen have claimed in their co-penned essay, 'There is no Alternative: THE FUTURE IS SELF ORGANISED', self-organisation is, amongst other things, 'a social process of communication and commonality based in exchange; sharing of similar problems, knowledge and available resources [4]'.

As a shared space for discussion, self-organisation enables a directed vocabulary to form based on one's own work. Every exhibition becomes a contingent moment in an evolution of a practice over time, where such momentary events function as self-regulated research tools for establishing links between practice as a space of negotiation beyond the individual position. Hopefully, these events also contribute to a more agile and self-empowering culture without the limitations of a decidedly fixed institutional structure.

From Conversation to the Formation of a Position

The artist Douglas Gordon once said that 'exhibitions are an excuse for a conversation' [5], but what Gordon's remark implies is that any moment of public display can initiate a potential space of dialogue among interested parties that only the event can set in motion. What Gordon highlights is a necessity for dialogue to move things forward, otherwise artistic practice remains in a self-imposed vacuum. Self-organised projects represent the difference between waiting for those moments of exchange to be initiated by outside forces instead of producing such moments alone.

Conversational modes of exchange are not without their own formal restraints or limitations. In fact, exhibition-moments, such as the private view or the after-opening pub session, can end up as the most formal of all discursive exchanges. Conversations are the first stage of exchange in a necessary move towards more formalised critique and modes of participation through which the potentiality for engagement with different publics, divergent readerships and diverse audiences can be widened beyond the mere convivial space of chatting. The transformation of the discursive space into forms of exhibition, public events, publications, public discussions and reading groups also enables the configuration of a useful social network, which enables the initiator to activate a potential space for a network to be called upon again in the future and for that network to grow over time.

From Invitee to Initiator

The invitation to take part in providing this text began with an email, followed by a conversational exchange. It was my ambition to maintain this mode of exchange for as long as was possible during the writing process. Thus, rather than immediately saying yes to the invitation and following instructions, I wanted to initiate an organisational process through which I could involve other voices instead of mediating solely on my own behalf. Having been given the opportunity by Visual Artists International (VAI) to write a text about organising one's own projects, this potential 'exhibition moment' became an opportunity to activate an exchange between a number of potential contributors.

The primary space of discourse, set in motion between VAI as the inviter and me as the invitee, became a secondary space of initiation. In turn, I asked 20 practitioners [6] whose work is often conditioned by self-organisational principles to respond to five rather oblique but open questions:

Why should we organise or initiate our own projects?

What are the benefits of self-initiated projects?

Is there a difference between taking part in self-organised projects and those that have been initiated by others?

What is self-determinism?

What is alternative cultural practice?

Their more than generous responses operated as the foundation for this text and wherever possible, their words are mediated here. Somewhat unsurprising, every respondent looked at self-initiated projects in a positive light. However, many appeared suspicious towards any fixed notion of what form these projects could take: projects for some might be organised due to urgent necessity, while others might pursue a level of organisation towards self-enterprise or establishment. As Pavel Büchler explained: '[Projects] can (but by no means necessarily do) manifest that things can be done differently in the face of concrete social, cultural or material situations. It goes without saying, then, that self-organisation is particularly meaningful where it is conceptually integral to the work, project or practice, rather than being merely a strategy for the dissemination of autonomous artworks or an exercise of entrepreneurial enterprise [7].

There is Always an Alternative

In 2005, Dave Beech and Mark Hutchinson curated the exhibition and publication 'There is Always an Alternative' at temporarycontemporary gallery space in Deptford, South London, which later toured to International 3 in Manchester. The exhibition proposed an alternative story about the period of artistic activity in the UK during the early 1990s – an alternate history to both the dominant story of Young British Artists (YBA) and the leading counter-narrative aligned to DIY artist-run space, such as City Racing and Bank, from which temporarycontemporary and International 3 are natural descendants. Rather than offer any grand narrative, Beech and Hutchinson proposed that many personal alternatives exist in regards to what passes as dominant cultural history. For instance, next to each artist's work at the exhibition, the pair hand-scribbled notes on the wall explaining how they had met the particular artist, what they were doing at the time and how they ended up working together.

'There is Always an Alternative' was not an alternative exhibition history in itself, but a proposition for the endless alternative accounts that make up cultural history. Without their initiation, such a narrative would remain untold, but it also enabled Beech and Hutchinson to insert their own practice into a meaningful framework without waiting for it to happen elsewhere. The need for a self-production of discourse around one's own practice is 'vital to control some aspects of the manifestation and dissemination of the artwork in the loosest and widest possible sense'[8]. Controlling this discourse at some level seems to be central to both Ele Carpenter and Ian Rawlinson's position in which they relate the ownership of one's ideas to the regulation of its reception where, 'the artistic principles of the work are contextualised, but not compromised in the process'[9]. Or, when artists 'are able to control the context in which the work is received to a greater extent through self-initiated projects... [and] the absence of an overbearing institutional agenda can allow some room for forms of production and distribution unavailable elsewhere'[10].

This urge to speak on one's own behalf in a self-generating manner is again mirrored in Pil and Galia Kollectiv's experience.

The best motivation for self-initiated projects is the desire to contextualise one's work. In the wake of the death of the author, we must ensure that viewers receive the best reading conditions. By placing our work alongside not only similar work, but work seemingly unrelated from other disciplines, we can create and influence the new meanings that emerge from the juxtaposition [11].

Self-initiated projects express an urgency to replace a lack of discourse around certain issues and provide an unbridled way into the processes behind one's own cultural operations. By initiating organisational activities, an artist, curator or writer expresses what Annie Fletcher called a 'need to see and discuss artistic practices or to manifest an idea through art which is not being manifested elsewhere' [12]. This reveals the possibility for a multitude of short-lived alternative perspectives and fosters a more horizontal critical space for shared enquiry among participants. Self-initiated projects also deduct the effects of an overly reliant culture that is dependant upon existing fixed institutional structures and conventional critical frameworks. As Pavel Büchler argues, such projects also 'differ from those initiated by institutions to the extent that they are expressions of an individually perceived sense of necessity, urgency or responsibility' [13]. These initiatives are all urgent and particular to each initiator, and can come in infinite guises that range from the artist who takes on a commission to fund a new body of work, to the curator who organises a show with a group of artists at a local market stall, to the writer who regularly pens letters to art magazines because of a lack of publishing outlets and eventually self-publishes the correspondence as a zine.

The artist, curator or writer may only wish to continue this type of work for a limited period before he or she moves on. However, it is the self-motivated act of 'doing' that remains fundamentally important and without which unknown possibilities can reveal themselves. In many ways, all cultural projects, regardless of their resistant origins, have an uneasy and habitually co-dependent relationship with established institutional structures and often necessitate their support at a future stage in order to move things forward. Not all self-organised projects are necessarily better than those initiated by institutions, but they do mediate some cultural discrepancy at any given moment for at least one member of that culture. Nor does the practice of self-organised projects mean that these activities provide any concrete alternative to existing power structures. However, they do suggest that the existing infrastructures are not to everyone's satisfaction and that there are always new ways of 'doing' and angles from which to see. These alternatives drive toward a more constantly shifting field of cultural production, echoed in an earlier text by Büchler, when he proposed that being an artist means:

'...Not doing different things than others do, but doing things differently [and] modern society needs creativity, critical imagination and resistance more than it needs works of art. It needs artists with their own ways of doing things more than it needs the things that they make. It needs the artists for what they are, rather than what they do, then it is in the sense in which artists are producers of culture rather than of discrete artefacts which characterise this culture' [14].

An example of Büchler's approach to thinking about artists for what they do rather than what they make, is apparent in the attitude of hospitality, a theme that often emerges in his projects. For example, the book *Conversation Pieces* was produced to accompany Büchler's 2003 exhibition at Tampere in Finland, in which nine practitioners (including John Stezaker, Simon Morris, Tim Brennan, Sharon Kivland and Will Bradley) were commissioned to produce a piece of writing in dialogue with Büchler's. However, the commissioned artists were asked only to use the act of writing about Büchler's work as a lens for viewing their own practice. Texts varied in style and approach, but the writers used the provided context to produce extensions of their own practice, not merely respond to Büchler's work.

A non-prescriptive invitation acts as a contemplative trigger for each of the contributors to reflect on their own work. The texts were simply a means to explore ideas, while the invitation served the artists as an excuse to produce something new for themselves. Infinite examples of such projects based on varying modes of the hospitality principle exist, where a two-way exchange between host and guest enables both the inviter and invitee to thrive.

Closer to home, numerous initiatives such as Via, Four Gallery, Feint zine and Pallas have taken hospitality as their central organising principle for accommodating local practice. Other variations on the theme of hosting have included Sarah Pierce's The Metropolitan Complex, Dublin, where Pierce holds informal meetings for local practitioners to discuss their concerns to understand her own. Afterwards, Pierce shares the the proceedings in a published newspaper format.

At 'Do Something For Floating IP' (2004), Manchester's artist-run space Floating IP, exhibited a project by artists Dave Beech and Graham Parker, who simply asked artists to submit something in the form of a proposal as a method of kick-starting the programme. There were no limitations, and all submissions were exhibited. Paul McAree and Mona Casey echoed the Manchester exhibition at the Colony Gallery space in Birmingham for the 2006 show, 'All at Once, Together, At the Same Time'. All artworks proposed as part of an open submission were accepted regardless of merit, as a means of establishing an artist network for the organisation. Finally, London's temporarycontemporary (a project of Jen Wu and Anthony Gross) takes an open curatorial approach to expansive exhibitions. The gallery shirks overarching thematic restraints in order to accommodate as many artists as possible within the expanding local and now international network.

Self-organisation undoes certain historical preconceptions towards notions of what roles an artist, critic or curator can take. As Dave Beech claims, 'it is about doing things on your own terms' and 'taking control of the means of distribution' that have an impact on the work, which can provide a mode of resistance to art's institutions and resist the conventions that artists make and critics and curators display. [15] Self-organisation also offers an alternative to art's institutions from which institutions themselves can learn and adopt, although at a different speed of engagement. If everyone waited for supportive assistance, the progress of culture would occur at a relatively fixed rate, whereby the inherent distribution of power would be maintained at a certain level from the top-down. As David Blamey states:

'It is important that some artists and curators organise their own projects. The art world relies upon independent producers to challenge its power base just as democracy flourished with a measure of dissent. As new ideas and practices are assimilated into the mainstream the prevalent culture of agreement is protected and the power base maintained'[16].

For James Hutchinson, the existing framework for cultural activity is always in flux. It is up to the artist or curator to recognise gaps in existing cultural frameworks and to generate new conversations and conventions for operation. In turn, these can be further subverted in that constantly shifting environment. Hutchinson describes culture gaps as 'alternative space', and he claims that 'once the gap is filled, it becomes part of the existing framework for other artists/curators (ie institutionalised)… and the gaps change all the time and new gaps form'. None of these can ever be completely filled at the same time [17]. Similarly, for Liam Gillick, the benefits of self-initiated projects lie in acknowledging that culture's gaps have great 'potential for absences; modes of refusal; excess or lacks of mediation; use of new spaces, geographies and proximities; avoidances of the validating processes of official culture'. Self-organised projects can 'question the established mediating structures that develop around cultural activity with specific instrumentalised aims that might run contrary to the critical potential of art now' [18].

In addition to gaps in culture, there are always gaps in one's personal knowledge. By establishing a way of working that employs knowledge-producing attributes learnt through self-organised projects, one can begin to think of those gaps as opportunities towards a self-education. David Goldenberg described the influence of his first self-initiated projects on the development of his later and more established practice:

'Self-initiated projects were seen as a possibility for developing a project completely on my own terms. I treated the construction and formulation of a project as an extension of my practice and thinking, where staging a project allowed the possibility for working through ideas for assembling and staging the different components of an exhibition. In other words, a project is a reflection of a complex understanding of how an exhibition is constructed and how one element is dependent on all the other elements. This led to a type of critical practice that tested out available positions and the limitations of the construction of the exhibition. This blurring of roles – where the artist and curator merge and a metaunderstanding of staging a project was developed

– corresponded [with an] understanding of [how] the methodology of a contemporary practice [could] provide the critical tools to dismantle and deconstruct the ideological construction of the traditions of modern art'[19].

Many of the responses to my questions mirrored Homi Bhabha's well worn statement, that 'in every emergency, there is an emergence'. What Goldenberg's self-determining response demonstrates is not just whether self-initiated projects are a necessary tool during periods of emergency in one's career, but also how, a more skilled, networked, informed and complete practice can emerge.

From initial idea to eventual completion, self-organised projects increase one's understanding of the complexities of artistic processes and stages of development. Alongside the knowledge that is gained through these experiences, one can begin to see how even the institution of culture itself is more of a long-term construction rather than a short-term fix.

Endnotes

1. Vaari Claffey later became co-director of MultiplesX in 1999.

2. See Mika Hannula's *Self-Organisation: A Short Story of a Family Tree* in Will Bradley et al, eds. Self-organisation/ Counter-Economic Strategies (Berlin, New York: Sternberg Press, 2006) pp 207.

3. Raymond Williams recognises three categories of usage for the term culture: '(i) the independent and abstract noun which describes a general process of intellectual, spiritual and aesthetic development, from C18; (ii) the independent noun, whether used generally or specifically, which indicates a particular way of life, whether of a people, a period, a group, or humanity in general...[and] (iii) the independent and abstract noun which describes the works and practices of intellectual and especially artistic activity." See Raymond Williams: *Keywords: A Vocabulary of Culture and Society* (London: Fontana Press, 1976) p 90.

4. See Anthony Davies, Stephan Dillemuth and Jakob Jakobsen's short text 'There is no Alternative: THE FUTURE IS SELF ORGANISED Part I' in Nina Möntmann, ed., *Art and its Institutions* (London: Black Dog Publishing, 2006) pp 176–178.

5. See Douglas Gordon, interviewed by Hans Ulrich Obrist, in *Hans Ulrich Obrist Interview Volume I* (Milan: Charta, 2003) pp 317–326.

6. Those invitees who kindly responded were: Adelaide Bannerman, Pavel Büchler, Shezad Dawood, Sam Ely & Lynn Harris, Charles Esche, Annie Fletcher, David Goldenberg, Cedar Lewishon, Dave Beech, David Blamey, Ele Carpenter, Gareth Phelan, Ian Rawlinson, James Hutchinson, Liam Gillick, Paul McAree, Pil and Galia Kollectiv.

7. Pavel Büchler in response to questionnaire.

8. Shezad Dawood in response to questionnaire.

9. Ele Carpenter in response to questionnaire.

10. Ian Rawlinson in response to questionnaire.

11. Pil and Galia Kollectiv in response to questionnaire.

12. Annie Fletcher in response to questionnaire.

13. Pavel Büchler in response to questionnaire.

14. From a paper delivered by Pavel Büchler at the Civic Arts Inquiry, City Art Centre, (Dublin, 2003).

15. Dave Beech in response to questionnaire.

16. David Blamey in response to questionnaire.
17. James Hutchinson in response to questionnaire.
18. Liam Gillick in response to questionnaire.
19. David Goldenberg in response to questionnaire.

In Support

Céline Condorelli

Support is based on generosity. It is critical, but support is not a category in itself; the act can be applied to work across other categories. Support can be defined as a type of relationship between people, objects, social forms and political structures. Each relationship proposes a specific mode and language of operation, and all open themselves towards further relations. Support promotes particular investigations in how we might work together towards change, and it becomes critical in allowing a form of political imagination to occur, as a position and practice. Support invites readings and inhabitations of relationships between power structures, social realities and institutional forms.

There are many forms of support, but nothing is inherently supportive, and nothing is inherently conflicting. Support can occur in the interstices of cultural structures or society – in its ad-hoc formations and encounters – but support largely exists with a 'for' that immediately follows. Although it is sometimes hard to recognise (as it takes a position of interface and organisation that inevitably recedes in the background), this prepositional add-on highlights that 'support' is a practice of weakness and negotiation. As such, the act functions through a language between the ad-hoc and the temporary [1].

Support allows us to think towards an equalising movement. It is a carrier for interdependency as a form of re-equalisation. The proposition of support is to transform what we produce by revisiting our modes of production. Through the practice of 'supporting,' we can rethink the very processes by which we operate. Defining a 'supportive relationship' points toward a different category for action, one that is concerned with how the political is staged and performed – its inherent ideology of frames [2] and display, organisational forms, appropriation, dependency and temporariness.

'The idea of generosity – and friendship – is central to this thought. To be a friend, in Derrida's terms one must know what it means to depend on a friend [3]. This is, at least metaphorically, the capacity of scaffolding that (Support Structure) references, as a protoarchitectural supposition. Again, and not without logic in Derrida's terms, this is incidentally a very redemptive idea.' (Andrea Philips, 'Doing Democracy')

Supporting contains an offer, an invitation. But first of all it establishes a relationship of inter-dependency, the entry into which is the opening up of potential communities, associations and active relationships. Supporting means engaging both political and hierarchical co-responsibility.

Beyond the conceptual level, how can forms of support be articulated on smaller levels of particular organisations, and how do they propose an alternative form of governance?

For instance, how does one define friendship? Dependency might be part of it; a reciprocal dependency may exist, as well as trust, choice, kindness and negotiation. Does support rely on friendship? Is offering support dependent on or synonymous with being a friend? Does friendship create the condition for support to occur? Or does support allow for the possibility of friendship?

According to Schmidtt, a friend is the one who is not an enemy, but this negative definition remains unsatisfactory towards the active practice of friendship. Friendship is not exclusively a relationship between individuals; it is a term used to characterise mutual assistance, trust and support, as well as a particular active involvement for a cause or principle. Friends of museums or organisations donate time or financial assistance – activities that incidentally also produce credibility for the individual and the organisation. This type of encouragement is different from that of charity because its aim is not directed towards the selfless gift (and possible consequential redemption) of one's belongings, but towards a level of identification with a cause or situation that is utilised in the process of individuation. A supporter, therefore, feels pleasure in an act towards his own autonomy and through this very act of supporting, be it emotional, ethical, practical or even philosophical. What can we apply from these observations towards a practice of support in the public realm?

One must start from the assumption that humans want or need to activate civil society as multiple political agencies. With this as a starting point, we can begin to reinvent democracy by expanding its spacial context in the public sphere. It is no longer possible to work towards the ideal of a unified

public sphere that addresses a single, self-governing community; the formations of public space that surround us impose a particular type of behavior that has only the semblance of an engagement in the public realm – it merely appears to possess an active participation in the political and in society. These participative modes are used as confirmations rather than expansions of the decision-making process and underline the urgency of re-democratising how we inhabit the public sphere.

What kinds of structures can allow us to imagine different types of engagements? Where is the space of 'appearance'? Through the practice of 'supporting', can we invent alternative institutions in support of a form of political imagination?

I, of course, cannot pretend to provide an answer, but can only test this hypothesis through practice and by raising new sets of questions. The first question concerns forms of top-down support in relation to the welfare state and its demise, and a re-democratisation through the bottom-up support that I am proposing. Enacting this type of generosity can only be done through particular strategies and methods of action. This is the moment when a paradox appears between the pure potential of a support structure and the bureaucratisation and institutionalisation of the very structures one needs to utilise. This is not as innocent or 'good' as it looks; through this process, the opening up of potential can also mean the destruction (or at least the profound questioning) of what is being supported. What I mean is that once possibilities for revision are open, the consequences are open as well, and can result in necessary closings and disappearances.

One example worth mentioning is Support Structure's project for the Portsmouth Multicultural Group, which was a perfect example of a small council organisation that embodied the problems (conflicting interests and ideologies) of a supporting government.

The project led the group to question not only its own identity, but also its place within the city and relationship with residents to such an extent that when several key members realised their ambitions and desires could never be fulfilled through the present organisational structure, they left the organisation and in essence declared the dismantling of some of the assumptions on which it was built. Events such as the one described can be understood as the destructive side of support. Despite the resulting disorganisation, they offer the possibility for questioning and therefore, closure.

Céline Condorelli

Superficially, support can be understood as an action aimed towards the fulfillment of a need – this translates to the notion, which I am very interested in, of the generalisation of individuals as 'subjects' in need. The citizen is transformed into the receptacle – someone or thing to which governmental structures and democratic processes are applied rather than an active force who partakes in the governing of the nation state. But of course we know that no relationship is one-sided, and that power, like any political relation, needs to be exercised by those in situations of apparent advantage – meaning that structures only exist through their process of activity. However, practising support in the context of smaller organisational levels, might allow us to think towards a mutually equalising process.

Yet, the question remains: what is being supported and through which means? Support structures offer possibilities beyond and sometimes against their initial invitation. What kind of a position does this represent?

I am not a political theorist, but I am interested in the type of practice that this proposes. Working in the cultural realm consists of an ongoing process of political positioning that engages, through its own mediums, language and discursive sites in the larger forces at work.

Negotiation can be understood as the opposite of principle. It is the most repressed element of the idea of democracy, as it inevitably contains some compromise, and compromise is usually seen as a declaration of weakness.

Negotiation offers a process for articulation, and the acknowledgement of antagonistic positions, in order to produce with effective modes of commonality – a being-in-common towards further dialogues and complexifications. A support structure is, in a sense, a questioning structure – a supplement, a somehow external organisation, at least with a certain autonomy from the situation it addresses; this allows it to pose, expose and revise questions in relationship to context and its operations. Support is negotiation. It is not the application of principle, but the conversation towards something that it does not define. The architectural construction of power is never in itself impermeable, but is rendered so by the institutions that install and maintain it, that support its condition or its coming into being. Therefore, the next question becomes, how do we negotiate with these objects and the institutions behind them?

In fact, it is culture that allows the individual to position him or herself in the public realm, amongst permanently shifting and conflicting inputs, the

conciliation of which is the making of public space. This means that a European political or non-political project must be formulated around a cultural structure as well as an economical one. The environments we inhabit are therefore embedded in this constant process of formulation and are negotiated by politics between the paradigms of culture and economics. This tractable dimension of the public realm is where we can measure our rights as citizens. By entering the public realm, one becomes part of the process of negotiation, which relies on multiple possibilities encouraged in the environment, rather than fixed positions. Negotiation might be one of the essential elements for a minimal framework for European civil rights [4].

The combination of culture, politics and economy can function as a tool and content – as object and site of artistic practice. These components are creative and interpretive practices. They are productions that take the form of negotiated relations between discourses and practices, between politics and culture.

Interrogating a discipline's relations to power structures and to social and territorial organisations is a necessary endeavor that anchors a work that is meant to access and put forth shared notions of space and negotiation (social, aesthetic, political). A contextual practice (this may be art or architecture) needs not only to construct and present a context, but it also must acknowledge itself as actively producing or fabricating the environment with which it engages. This transformation of the understanding of context, and therefore of the context itself, from a set of conditions to a political production, is to inscribe it with a new set of possibilities; what is identified are not simply formal or architectural interventions, but implicit connections, visible or invisible, to the potential organisation and operation of structures of power and control.

The landscape of cultural production is the site of such a practice, and temporariness, dependency and invisibility are the tools suggested by support. Here, work is organised around the creation of alternative loci for speech and action.

It was of course Foucault who said, in his famous interview with Paul Rabinow [5], that the forces of global political processes remain invested in architecture. Despite its predictability, this statement is important not merely because it articulates the active relationship of architecture and power. Instead, it opens the possibility for architecture to be thought and exercised anew, differently, again and again. From conceiving it as belonging to inescapable orders of liberation or oppression, Foucault liberated spatial form, and with it the practice of architecture. An architecture of oppression might be one of the elements that makes resistance and opposition possible, but it is not in the architecture itself that liberation from oppression is contained or embodied: 'liberty, is a practice…liberty is what must be exercised.'

Architecture might be able to support a form of political institution and vice versa, but it cannot control or determine it. It can, however, cause material and formal differentiations. Still, it is the other institutions that support that physical condition – that actually establish the political space.

The political space depends on both physical and conceptual forms, but also on the context, spatial, political, temporal attitudes. At best, architecture controls some aspects of material form, and it participates in producing political space. We need other institutions to prop up (or support) the architectural effect; the notion of propping up is where a certain mythology about architecture and its making contradicts the notion of autonomy. Architecture could install a democracy, or any other forms of organisation, depending on the kinds of institutions, military, economic, or social patterns that support it in the first place. In turn, the architecture supports the institution, and produces it; it stages the political and with it the inherent ideology of frames.

Architecture, or any spatial form, comes into being through supporting institutions, which expose all the problems of thinking of art or architecture as applied practices in relationship to a need or lack. The ideal of autonomy is pulling away from the inherent messiness of intervening in the social realm – working away from independence towards notions of equity and interdependency – and is profoundly concerned with a certain type of invisibility.

This is the invisibility of permanence and image, an actively promoted incapacity to articulate any kind of final product. Support maintains possibilities open to collapse as well as eventual repair (a making perfect again, back to a mythical original state) or transformation. Temporariness is a means of resistance to the occurrence of a solution, it pushes the predictability of an outcome away by stretching its own weakness, therefore allowing a state of possibility (or status quo) to further remain open.

There is in the practice of supporting, a movement towards the erasure of the visible, encouraging a non-articulated visuality in order to precisely never arrive at any possible conclusion or solution by even attempting to provide an image of it, which could be defined as a form of blindness. This 'imagination' is replaced by the process of construction, production, and desire, through

uncertainty, generosity and negotiation. This is the process that forms the public realm. Through it, democracy occurs. Although support constantly evolves, it becomes essential to make the processes of practice tangible, through asking questions, giving voice, constructing frameworks and platforms, making invitations and, of course, by offering support.

Endnotes

This essay was published on the 2007 launch of *Ahali: a journal for setting a setting.*

1. Temporariness

Scaffolding and other forms of support seem temporary even though they might appear over long periods of time. Rather than holding something together in order to allow it to support itself, making it whole (which would appear to be its very first *raison d'être*), the presence of support prolongs a moment of crisis. Support instead reveals the occurrence of a point of jeopardy and ruptures the autonomy of the object; it exposes the now inherently incomplete state of the supported object, as well as the somewhat inappropriate and fragile nature of scaffolding.

2. 'Richardson 358 A frame is essentially constructed and therefore fragile: such would be the essence or truth of the frame, if it had any ... But what has produced and manipulated the frame puts everything to work in order to efface the frame effect.' – Jacques Derrida, *The Truth in Painting*

3. 'He had gone barely half a mile when he met a lame Fox and a blind Cat, walking together like two good friends. The lame Fox leaned on the Cat, and the blind Cat let the Fox lead him along, so that no one knew who was helping whom.' – Carlo Collodi, *The Adventures of Pinocchio*

4. See Bart de Baere, 'Leviathan revised'.

5. Paul Rabinow, May 1984, just before Foucault's death. Translation by Lydia Davis, Vol. 1, 'Ethics' of *Essential Works of Foucault*, (The New Press 1997).

All images:
Céline Condorelli, Support Structures, (after Adam Broomberg and Oliver Chanarin) 2007

e+l

Ken Ehrlich and Brandon LaBelle

e+l stages investigative performances based on urban infrastructures and spatial scenarios, such as food, transport and waste management systems. This has resulted in past projects in the cities of Hull (UK), Berlin and recently in Curitiba, Brazil. Including research and empirical surveying, the projects seek to map infrastructures – some of which are more clearly marked than others – through discursive and performative actions. The projects question our individual ability to access governmental information; to interview and understand greater city policies and their impact on societal behaviours; to gauge local cultures; and to apply what we know to bring forward a creative intervention on these infrastructures to reveal critical perspectives.

41

The movement of goods is housed within a larger infrastructure of roadways, transport, manufacturing and consumption – an entire system of mechanism of handling. The image of the truck comes to symbolise the larger economy and also operates within a cultural and psychic landscape. The truck is a matrix for the generative making of open-road fantasies of freedom and loss, and in particular, the macho-trucker and the bravado of raw energy. Trucking travels both ways, as a productive vehicle operating within a sphere of supply and demand, and a slippery signifier adding to the momentum that defines the road as a pure potential.

42

How might we trace the shifting economies between capital and desire? Where do we locate the intersection and slippages occurring between production and consumption and their related by-products? In highway spaces, we imagine narratives of 'Free Trade' intersecting with *Easy Rider*. multiple narratives mark the road both as a site for more cultural and economic activity. The labour of the trucker, the mechanics of trucks and the workings of dispatchers and related transport companies feature as efficient systems always on the edge of disruption, distraction, and delay, according to the complications of labouring bodies fixated on the roadway. The trucker comes to occupy the site also via midnight adventures, vehicular daydreams and escapist moments in life.

The roads remain a complex and conflicted site, where the interstate system as public space theoretically facilitates travel and transport according to the rhythm of capital, while the mythology of the highway runs throughout culture as a conduit of free expression. The highway becomes a space of pure fantasy – 'as we rolled in Iowa City he saw another truck coming behind us, and because he had to turn off at Iowa City he blinked his tail lights at the other guy and slowed down for me to jump out, which I did with my bag, and the other truck, acknowledging this exchange, stopped for me, and once again, in the twink of nothing I was in another big high cab, all set to go hundreds of miles across the night and I was happy!...'(J Keuroac). In the space of mystic highway narratives, the practicalities of movement and transportation are juxtaposed with the performative disgressions of individual will and imagination. To get behind the wheel then is to enter a system of banal functionality and also the potentiality for total oblivion.

Cavite Export Processing Zone

Dirk Fleischmann

I was in Rosario in May 2007 to prepare for a project about the fashion industry. I followed the traces of Naomi Klein who visited Rosario in 1997. She describes the working conditions in this area in her book, No Logo.

I revisited all places and people that Naomi Klein mentions in the chapter about Rosario, Cavite. In my search I was interested what has changed in the past 10 years and what information in the book is still valid. Additionally, it helped me to find out about the city and the export production zone to get a comprehensive overview of the current situation.

You can see a selection of the photos of my research here. All quotes are taken from Klein's No Logo and the photos relate to the quotes.[1]

In March 2008, I produced a shirt as a mass product in one of the factories in the Cavite Export Processing Zone. The complete project is documented on the website, myfashionindustries.com.

45

'If Niketown and the other superstores are the glittering new gateways to the branded dream worlds, then the Cavite Export Processing Zone, located 90 miles south of Manila in the town of Rosario, is the branding broom closet... Rosario's population of 60,000 all seemed to be on the move; the town's busy, sweltering streets were packed with army jeeps converted into minibuses and with motorcycle taxis with precarious sidecars.'

'Its sidewalks lined with stalls selling fried rice, Coke and soap...Most of this commercial activity serves the 50,000 workers who rush through Rosario on their way to and from work in the zone, whose gated entrance is located smack in the middle of town.'

'Inside the gates, factory workers assemble the finished products of our branded world: Nike running shoes, Gap pajamas, IBM computer screens, Old Navy jeans.'

'Their names and logos aren't splashed on the façades of the factories in the industrial zone... And here, competing labels aren't segregated each in its own superstore; they are often produced side by side in the same factories, glued by the very same workers, stitched and soldered on the very same machines.'

Cavite Export Processing Zone

Dirk Fleischmann

'The streets in the zone are eerily empty, and open doors – the ventilation system for most factories – reveal lines of young women hunched in silence over clamoring machines.'

'All the bustle and color of Rosario abruptly stops at the gates, where workers must show their UD cards to armed guards in order to get inside... Buses and taxicabs must drop their speed and silence their horns when they get into the zone – a marked change from the – boisterous streets of Rosario.'

48

'When I climb up the water tower on the edge of the zone and look down at the hundreds of factories, it seems as if the whole cardboard complex could lift up and blow away, like Dorothy's house in *The Wizard of Oz*'.

'But walk out of the gate and the bubble bursts. Aside from the swarms of workers at the start and end shifts, you'd never know that the town of Rosario is home to more than 200 factories. The roads are a mess, running water is scarce and garbage is overflowing.'

'Many of the workers live in shantytowns on the outskirts of town and in neighbouring villages.'

'Others, particularly the youngest workers, live in the dormitories, a hodgepodge of concrete bunkers separated from the zone enclave by only a thick wall. The structure is actually a converted farm, and some rooms, the workers tell me, are really pigpens with roofs slapped on them.'

'Jose Ricafrente has the dubious honour of being mayor of Rosario...I met with him in his small office, while a lineup of needy people waited outside...A once-modest fishing village, his town today has the highest per capita investment in all of the Philippines – thanks to the Cavite zone – but it lacks even the basic resources to clean up the mess that the factories create in the community.'

'Rosario has all the problems of industrialisation – pollution, an exploding population of migrant workers, increased crime, rivers of sewage – without any of the benefits.'

'There are rules against talking, and at the Ju Young electronics factory, a rule against smiling.'

'One of the reasons I went to Cavite is that I had heard this zone was a hotbed of trouble making, thanks to a newly formed organisation called the Workers' Assistance Center...Attached to Rosario's Catholic church only a few blocks from the zone's entrance, the center is trying to break through the wall of fear that surrounds free-trade zones in the Philippines.'

'In Cavite, you can't talk about overtime without the conversation turning to Carmelita Alonzo, who died, according to her co-workers… of overwork.'

'Raymondo Nagrampa, the zone administrator, acknowledged that it would certainly be better if the factories hired more people for fewer hours, but he told me, 'I think I will leave that I think this is more of a management decision?'…The group of workers gathered around the table at the Workers' Assistance Center burst out laughing when I asked them about job security or a guaranteed number of working hours. 'No work, no pay!' the young men and women exclaim in unison.'

'All through the Asian zones, the roads are lined with teenage girls in blue shirts, holding hands with their friends and carrying umbrellas to shield them from the sun.

'Cecille Tuico, one of the organisers at the Workers' Assistance Center, was listening in on the conversation. After the workers left to make their way through Rosario's dark streets and back to the dormitories, she pointed out that the alienation the workers so poignantly describe is precisely what the employers look for when they seek out migrants instead of locals to work in the zone.'

All excerpts are from Naomi Klein, *No Logo* (Canada: Alfred A Knopf, 2000).

The Virtual World Needs to be Shared in the Streets

Interview with the Mosireen Collective

Emanuele Guidi with Jasmina Metwaly

EMANUELE GUIDI: You define yourself as 'a non-profit media collective born out of the explosion of citizen journalism and cultural activism'. How did you exactly get to the decision of founding Mosireen collective and what was your relationship with the 2011 revolution?

MOSIREEN: During the 18 days the eyes of the news channels were bird-viewing over Tahrir, the most interesting footage showing what was really happening was made by people on the ground, filming, what was around them. I spent the 18 days filming, and sometimes I wish I wasn't and just sat down. But I had this urgency to capture, so I would have something to remember for later. Mosireen came about in a response to this urgency. We wanted to create a platform that would support citizens, armed with cameras and mobile phones, to continue on building the archive of the events and share it with the whole world. The idea began in the aftermath of the 9 March, 2011 events; we witnessed soldiers and thugs enter the square, beating people with electric cables and sticks. The tortures continued later on in the museum where the military would put civilians in front of the tribunal. It was a bloody night, which for many was a clear signal that the army and SCAF (Supreme Council of Military Forces) should not be trusted. The group, No to Military Trials on Civilians, learned this from Amr El Beheiry, who was captured earlier in February and was initially sentenced to five years in prison. Those military trials on civilians were already happening in January that year. We had a lot of testimonies, but no clear footage showing the army beating and taking people away, so 9 March was a breaking point, and it enabled us to uncover SCAF's violations towards civilians. The abuses of the past caught up with the present, allowing the military to get away with impunity. My realisation after last year is that the revolution needs to continue.

55

EMANUELE GUIDI: Can you describe how you work? How did you begin to collect the material that the people were filming with their mobile phones and cameras? How did you make yourself known in Cairo and in other cities in Egypt?

MOSIREEN: There were several things happening simultaneously. There was the archived material that was being organised to be accessible to people. Parts were collected by the media tent during the 18 days and it grew into something much bigger over time. Now, it is more organised, and people can pass by Mosireen to share their footage. The sources vary depending on the nature of the issue filmed and the tool used. When there are clashes in the streets we are all down, filming in groups and then editing and uploading as fast as possible. During the Mohamed Mahmoud clashes in November, I spent a lot of time filming at the hospitals, mostly in Kasr El Ainy, where we discovered that a lot of the injured protesters were shot in the head by security forces. These accounts were urgent and crucial to depict the military and security forces crimes.

Whatever is happening in the streets, the most popular device used is a mobile phone, but people also use flip cams, camcorders, SLRs…depending on the budget. We go to places to conduct interviews ourselves and film a particular situation that needs to be recognised. Later on we edit the material into a more layered and longer video. We also organise training and workshops in Cairo and in other cities. The idea is to help others learn the necessary skills to conduct an interview or create a short video and upload it online or organise a screening. This way the collective grows, allowing individuals and groups to speak about their local issues and problems in their own neighbourhoods.

EMANUELE GUIDI: From the video-making and video-editing to YouTube channels and all the other social media, can you describe your relationship with the Internet as a platform to spread information worldwide?

MOSIREEN: Social media allows you to quickly share information with hundreds and thousands of people simultaneously. People can watch and download films through the Mosireen YouTube channel. Videos in higher resolution, suitable for screenings can be downloaded from Vimeo. The internet is a useful tool to spread information, but it also has its limitations. People without access cannot see most of the videos that are being shared through social media platforms (ie Twitter, Facebook etc). The virtual world needs to be shared in the streets.

This is why we started organising public screenings and distributing CDs containing our material and videos.

EMANUELE GUIDI: One of the practices that interests me the most and that defines your way of acting are the temporary open-air cinemas in Tahrir Square and in other parts of the city. Through this action you reconnect the virtual 'public' space with the actual 'public' space of the city. Could you describe how you organize them and the importance of these gatherings as social moments?

MOSIREEN: The virtual becomes the actual, in a sense that the audience is confronted with the reality and experiences in a 1:1 scale. I remember a screening in Tahrir where we showed the video with the army clearing the square on 9 March. People were watching something that had happened in the same place, just a month earlier. What happened is that the very subjective violence became objective in a way that hadn't been seen before by people. Tahrir Cinema started in the square, but has now moved and is happening everywhere, through *Kazeboon* ('liars' in Arabic) screenings for instance, which is a public awareness campaign that started in response to the crimes depicted by the military. *Kazeboon* takes place everywhere; videos are being screened on the walls of buildings, in the streets of neighbourhoods where people do not necessarily have access to the internet. Basically information by itself is not active and it needs an element that activates it, lets it free. So being a cyberpunk is not enough, because making something available does not necessarily make it active. To have access to knowledge is a privilege, and we need to remember not to underestimate the power of the physical, human confrontation that goes beyond the screen.

EMANUELE GUIDI: So this 'sharing' process on line and in the square was, and still is, the precondition for people to become not only more aware but also more autonomous and independent in their actions. Do you have an example of some form of action or mobilisation that was the result of this information process?

MOSIREEN: It is hard to tell. For instance the video testimony of Aboudi, who was tortured at the Cabinet in December, 2011, had a lot of hits. I believe that it made an impact on people and encouraged them to join the protest, yet it is very hard to measure it more precisely. We previously made videos that were a call for action, but a lot of them did not get enough views to have a direct influence. I think that image resistance plays an important role in this, but it is only one of the elements that creates reaction. Actions erupt and cannot be designed. People's response to information sometimes takes time and so does action or mobilisation.

<u>EMANUELE GUIDI</u>: How do you feel your work is perceived in Europe and in the rest of the world? Are we just an 'audience' or are there other forms of exchange and relationships?

<u>MOSIREEN</u>: Both. Sometimes you hear a question from the audience: 'So what can we do?' There's only so much one can do, but people should start with their own governments, see what their policies are and how the decision-making process happens under a veil of spreading democracy. People support us in different ways. From subtitling to organising screenings and talks. There are many platforms that share our videos and work on supporting Mosireen. We have just launched our Indiegogo crowdsourcing campaign. So please support us if you can.

For more information: http://mosireen.org

Photograph Sherief Gaber

Dehors

Haegue Yang

2006
Slide projection, looped. Two sets of 81 colour slides each, two slide projectors, dissolve control
Photograph: Haegue Yang, Courtesy of Galerie Wien Lukatsch, Berlin

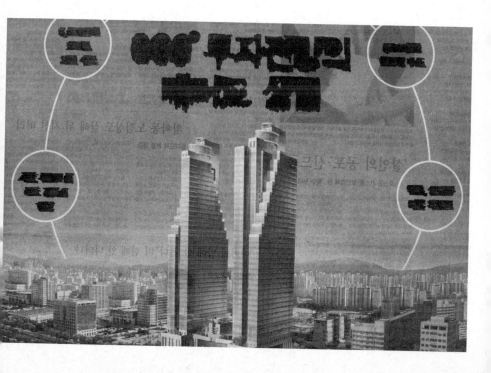

Model-Making

Propositions, Regulations, Patterns, Enthusiasms

Museum

72 South 8 street #6, Brooklyn, New York
Drawn 1994 Re-drawn 2007

Nils Norman

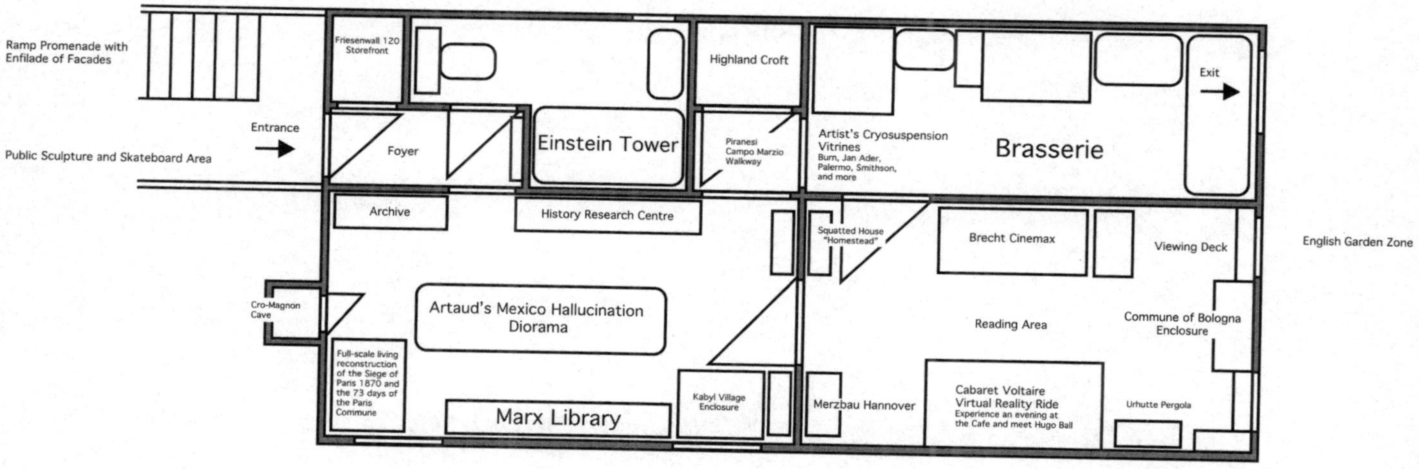

museum. 72 South 8th street #6, Brooklyn, NY

English Garden Zone

Exit

Brasserie

Viewing Deck

Commune of Bologna Enclosure

Urhutte Pergola

Brecht Cinemax

Reading Area

Cabaret Voltaire
Virtual Reality Ride
Experience an evening at
the Cafe and meet Hugo Ball

Artist's Cryosuspension
Vitrines
Burri, Jan Ader,
Palermo, Smithson,
and more

Squatted House
"Homestead"

Merzbau Hannover

Highland Croft

Pronesi
Campo Marzio
Walkway

Kabyl Village
Enclosure

Einstein Tower

History Research Centre

Artaud's Mexico Hallucination
Diorama

Marx Library

Friesenwall 120
Storefront

Foyer

Archive

Full-scale living
reconstruction
of the Siege of
Paris 1870 and
the 73 days of
the Paris
Commune

Cro-Magnon
Cave

Entrance

Ramp Promenade with
Enfilade of Facades

Public Sculpture and Skateboard Area

Proposition for Reclaiming a Space

Bik Van der Pol

Mediation of ideas and creating a network of a growing circle of friends motivated the thinking behind 'Proposition for Reclaiming a Space' (1997), a reconstruction of the first gallery of Konrad Fischer that opened in the 1960s in Dusseldorf's Neubruckstrasse. The work is based on the simple gesture of creating, from an in-between space, a new and open space by installing two glass doors on both sides. For example, an alley can be used both to transport goods and allow people entrance to buildings in the backyard. This reconstruction presents the possibilities of creating and giving room, where artists, instead of the objects, play the central role in its development.

This attitude is based on trust, and with that in mind, Bik Van der Pol created an open empty space, thus giving the opportunity to revive, re-experience and review the actual space as well as the myth. George Jappe's 1971 interview with Konrad Fischer, published in *Studio International*, was reprinted as a folder (and for this occasion made as a reprint of a reprint) and placed in the space made available to the public. The later-developed 'Unlimited Edition' of this work, modeled at 1:1 scale, accompanied a simple explanation and building instructions. The project itself referred to the continuous optimism and trust in the function of art as a catalyst for change.

dispatch 036

E
selectors
A
NICHOLAS
LOGSDAIL
S
TACITA
DEAN
T
International

NORWICH GALLERY NORWICH SCHOOL OF ART AND DESIGN

St George Street Norwich Norfolk NR3 1BB

Telephone 01603 610561 Fax 01603 615728

nor.gal@nsad.ac.uk http://www.nsad.ac.uk/gallery/index.htm

SAINSBURY CENTRE FOR VISUAL ARTS UNIVERSITY OF EAST ANGLIA

Norwich NR4 7TJ Telephone 01603 456060 Fax 01603 259401

scva@uea.ac.uk http://www.uea.ac.uk/menu/organisation/scva

LIESBETH BIK & JOS VAN DER POL

Proposition for Reclaiming a Space *1997*

Mixed Media 345 x 250 x 850 cm

KONRAD FISCHER *interviewed by* **GEORG JAPPE**

Studio International vol 181 February 1971 pp 68 to 71

Exhibitions at Konrad Fischer Gallery Düsseldorf

First one-man shows	*Darboven (G) December 67*
	Sandback (USA) May 68
	Long (GB) September 68
	Fulton (GB) June 69
	McLean (GB) September 69
	Gilbert and George (GB) May 70
	Ruthenbeck (G) March 68
First European one-man shows	*Andre (USA) November 67*
	Artschweger (USA) June 68
	LeWitt (USA) January 68
	Nauman (USA) July 68
	Ryman (USA) December 68
	Smithson (USA) January 69
	Weiner (USA) April 69
	Huebler (USA) January 70
	Wilson (USA) October 70
First German one-man shows	*Dibbets (Hol) August 68*
	Rinke (G) March 69
	Buren (F) October 69
	Merz (I) March 70
	Law (GB) August 70
One-man shows in museums, arranged by Konrad Fischer	*Andre Darboven (Museum Mönchengladbach); Long, Sandback, LeWitt, Dibbets (Museum Haus Lange, Krefeld); Palermo (Museum Wuppertal Studio).*
Collective exhibitions arranged by Konrad Fischer	*'Prospect 68' and 'Prospect 69', Städtische Kunsthalle, Düsseldorf; 'Konzeption-Conception', Städtisches Museum Leverkusen, October 69.*
Other exhibitions	*Becher, Palermo, Polke, Richter, Rückriem (G); Bochner, Flavin, Marden (USA); Sladden (GB); Panamarenko (B)*

The young art dealer Konrad Fischer, born in 1939, started his first gallery in Düsseldorf only three years ago, and he is regarded as one of the most influential 'art agents' in any context involving new tendencies on the international art scene. The interview brings out, on the one hand, his novel method of working - investing ideas instead of capital - and on the other his marked personal style, which involves a concern with artists instead of their works (which may in any case already have been sold). Apart from giving an impression of Konrad Fischer's personality and ideas, what he says also raises questions of art politics. For example this is the first time, to my knowledge, in today's much expanded art world, that the demand for a precise division of labour between artist, dealer, public exhibition and museum has been not only raised but spelled out in detail.

Konrad Fischer has asked not to be represented by a photograph of himself, or by photographs from his exhibitions ('they're just random installation photos, things of the past'), but by a montage of his invitation cards. The use of picture postcards as private view invitations, which also serve as a record of the gallery's work and the artists who exhibit them, is regarded by Konrad Fischer as one of his inventions.

JAPPE *Didn't you start off as an artist?*

FISCHER Yes, I studied and painted at the Düsseldorf Academy, when was that, 1958-62. In 1963 I had my first show, at Schmela's, the *Sportsman* pictures. The best known thing, as you say, was the *Phosphorescent Shadow Play*, because the museums passed it around a bit. But I wouldn't waste much time on that, it's unimportant.

JAPPE *Why?*

FISCHER Because the art I produced is unimportant. 'What you are, Konny lad, is a good dealer', Schmela used to say. He forced the issue by asking me to start a second Schmela gallery for young people. I wasn't too keen, but everything happened very quickly. I was thinking it all out already; and it didn't work out quite as Schmela had imagined it. You see, I decided - I didn't need any money. What I had was less than 5000 marks - I went on teaching for a year after that - and an idea. Minimal art wasn't known in Europe, and I saw an opening. I thought it was important, and I knew it only from photographs. So I thought I'd try to get through to the artists - I was one myself after all - and I said to myself, 'If someone sends them a plane ticket, they'll come.' So I sent one to Andre.

JAPPE *Did you know him?*

FISCHER No, but his response was 'At last, someone wants to do a room with me.'

JAPPE *Giving artists a ticket and getting them to come, instead of spending a lot of money on transporting objects - was that your idea?*

FISCHER I never heard of anyone having the idea earlier. At least, those who have been given the credit were later than I was. My gallery opened in November 1967. After the Andre exhibition I didn't need to say anything; Andre said it for me. He said, 'Go right ahead it's great'. I have never corresponded much, and I have never worked with galleries much. Sol LeWitt came here quite independently of Dwan. The American galleries didn't make difficulties; the initial difficulties came from German dealers trying to make trouble with their colleagues in New York. I went to America for the first time in April 1968, and called people up - not Warhol or Lichtenstein, that's not interesting, but Judd. In his studio I discovered Sandback. I split the cost of my air fare with the Munich dealer Friedrich; since then like-minded galleries have often shared my expenses.

JAPPE *When you discover completely new people, how do you go about it?*

FISCHER I rely on a feeling. I have a strong conviction that I know what is good, otherwise I couldn't work. What I do is emotional and personal. When I have no information of my own to go on, I rely on the judgement of my friends, especially the artists. For example: I once had to put off a show with Sol LeWitt, and he recommended the drawings of a German girl who lived in New York, called Hanne Darboven. I did hastily find a replacement of my own, but it turned out to be unnecessary. There is no doubt that good artists respect other good artists, and yet there are so many utterly different personalities, in Minimal and Conceptual Art for example, that it doesn't lead to the formation of a clique. I owe a lot to these personal contacts; and chance has played a big part as well. When I was still an artist I shared an exhibition with Richard Long and Jan Dibbets at the Galerie Loehr in Frankfurt. I have never felt so spontaneously enthusiastic about anyone as I did about Richard Long. He had been at art school with George, of Gilbert and George. And Gilbert came from South Tyrol, and an exhibition held by my colleague Friedrich in Munich made him decide to go to art school in London. That shows that dealers with their exhibitions can do more than just show what is new; they are part of the process of producing it. On the other hand, when something gets recommended to me, and I have a feeling that I don't understand it - as with Kosuth's texts - then I leave it alone. And when he puffs himself up in *Studio International*, that's the sort of thing I can't take. The most important test is the exhibition itself. Of course you have a big advantage over the collector or the critic, when you stay with the stuff for a whole month. Sometimes I come home after setting up an exhibition and say 'Great, the best I've ever had!' And then a month later I see there's nothing to it at all. It's better to move gradually from scepticism to enthusiasm than the other way round. Of course there are some enthusiasms that last, but quite aside from enthusiasm, the momentary spark, I have set out to promote a single tendency, and not to keep a general store. If you specialize you can be clearer about the way to go.

JAPPE *Can you outline what this single tendency is?*

FISCHER To start with it was a new tendency that no one knew about in Europe, Minimal Art, and then it was the consequences that came from that: an abstract, reduced, serial art. Conceptual Art above all.

JAPPE *Although you represent a kind of art that the public finds uncongenial, you have become one of the best-known dealers in Germany because you have had an effect on the artistic climate as a whole. What were the considerations that guided you?*

FISCHER There is no gallery in Düsseldorf that is less well-known than mine. Twelve hundred people get my mail shots every month, but over three years there have been, at most, a thousand visitors to my gallery. I am unequivocally an 'in' gallery. And I am dead against 'education'- that's a job for a public institution.

JAPPE *And your job?*

FISCHER To get artists over here, and to bring them into contact with those who live here. When I was an artist everything was so far away; Warhol, Lichtenstein and all those were unattainable great men. But when you know them, you can have a beer with them and get rid of your inferiority complex. I insist that the artist has to be there when I show his work. A lot has been done in the last few years. Palermo and Richter, for example, two of the German artists who have exhibited with me, have now been to New York, and they felt at home there because they had already met artists like Andre and LeWitt over here. In the same way, the Americans go back and tell everyone that there are artists over here too. It's not the artists who are chauvinists, but the institutions.

JAPPE *But for the 'Prospect' show you brought whole galleries over as well?*

FISCHER For the first one, yes. At the second one it was mainly artists. At the Cologne Kunstmarkt only German dealers were allowed to take part. It would have been really informative if they had shown what was not known in this country, instead of pandering to chauvinism. The Kunstmarkt is a place to find out about prices, not about art. Strelow was well known in Düsseldorf as a journalist, and persuaded the city that 'Prospect' was the best and most economical way of providing an informative international survey of the latest tendencies in art. This is quite right; the trouble with a gallery is that the exhibitions come one after the other, there are no visible tie-ups, no direct juxtaposition, and yet different tendencies do have a lot in common. I can't sell anything that I am not convinced about. A museum, on the other hand, can provide the whole spectrum of information without having to engage its own responsibility with respect to all the artists individually.

JAPPE *Your German colleagues have criticized you on the grounds that 'Prospect' lured the collectors away from the German art market.*

FISCHER Practically nothing was sold at 'Prospect', there wasn't any poaching of clients, and anyway the big collectors are known internationally.

JAPPE *Yes, but in that case why did the American galleries come? They had to bear nearly all the costs themselves.*

FISCHER I am absolutely certain that it's important to the Americans galleries to have a progressive image in Europe. In America this image hardly exists at all; in Europe there are much better galleries, as far as courage and progressiveness are concerned. In America the galleries are basically general stores. Anything new is just a drop in the ocean. Friedrich, Sperone, Ricke, Art & Project, Wide White Space and I are way ahead of any American gallery from the point of view of consistent progressiveness. just look at Dwan or Castelli; they have six or eight shows a year, and the regulars just come back again and again. I just couldn't afford the variations in quality; in Europe blunders can be overlooked, but they're not forgotten. There is no doubt that there is a lot more progressiveness in Europe, and progressive art gets a response much more readily here than in America. In New York - apart from Seth Siegelaub, who's a private entrepreneur - there is no gallery accessible to the public that has shown Conceptual Art. I don't see any point in the progressive American artists moving to Europe; but I do believe that I think this is the place where they have an interest in finding out what they can do away from their own context.

JAPPE *Do you believe that progressive European art is growing in importance?*

FISCHER Definitely. In the last few years more and more good people from Europe have turned up and been recognized by the American artists, and that's something that didn't happen before. I'd like to make it quite clear that by this I don't mean Beuys. He is the best-known European artist, but in America they think he's a young man. He is possibly the most important artist of the post-war period, but he isn't young and over there they identify him with the rise of Process Art in 1968. If Beuys doesn't want to do an exhibition in America, Castelli would only have to put one together out of Beuys objects from the Kunstmarkt; but they're too expensive for him. Over there people think Beuys is just some new European artist, whereas he's really a classic.

JAPPE *So when you talk of young artists who do you mean?*

FISCHER Of the young artists from Europe who have gained recognition in America, the first ones I think of are Richard Long, Hanne Darboven, Daniel Buren, Jan Dibbets, and Gilbert and George. They were on show at major international events like the 'Attitudes' show in Berne and the Tokyo Biennale, and next year they will be represented in a central position in New York - but I don't want to talk about that yet. Richard Long now has a contract with Dwan. He had his first one-man show at my Gallery in September 1968.

JAPPE *How is it possible to establish an artist and to keep him going with limited financial resources?*

FISCHER The artists get their plane tickets, they stay with me - that's why I have such a large flat. The material costs are low. When I find an artist I can't start thinking about who is going to buy. To start with I did try a few times to have a specific buyer in mind, as dealers usually do. But I was never right. I made a fool of myself. Really. No gift for it. I'm not going to call up some collector and talk him into something. Things don't sell all that fast anyway. Although if I hadn't sold anything at the Andre show, I shouldn't have got much further. The first collectors were a Dutch couple, the Vissers. I haven't got many clients - a doctor, a bank director, a foundry engineer - and a few in Italy, Benelux and England. But more than 50% of what I sell goes to other galleries. Perhaps I'm not an ordinary art dealer. I'm not interested in this whole gallery business. I want to convey information, to show artist's work; I couldn't care less where I do it. I have never put a notice in a paper. I'd rather do museum exhibitions which are linked with my name. There's hardly a single big exhibition that's not put on with my help. Think of 'Attitudes' or the Conceptual Art show at Leverkusen, or the Haus Lange shows, to mention only those near here. The capital as far as the artists and I are concerned, is the publicity. What's important for me is not how to sell things but how to get information across to those who are interested, so that in due course the artists I represent get somewhere, and people say, 'Fischer got the right man'. I think the usual dealer's attitude, neglecting everything that has nothing to do with sales, is absolutely wrong. I see myself as an art agent; this is a long-term job, you have to build up gradually, it's no use expecting to get what you want in three years.

JAPPE *What are your plans for the future?*

FISCHER On that I want to say something basic. I don't believe it's possible, at the present moment, to interest a larger public than exists already. I think experiments like Street Art are a mistake. The idea is to present art to the public as entertainment, but there is no such thing as entertaining art - apart from a few of the by-products. The idea of bringing the museums up to date is based on a misconception. It's certainly possible to do up-to-date exhibitions; but sugaring the pill - music, advertising, and so on - is just a way of increasing the number of visitors. Museums are an archive of visual art. And when a museum puts on an exhibition of contemporary art it ought to do so in a museum-like way, that is, logically and coherently. Extending a tradition into the future: that's the way a museum ought to inform the public it ought to raise the value of tradition, through bringing in new tendencies, and not depreciate it as usually happens nowadays. A Minimal exhibition, for example, would make sense in the context of a Mondrian and Bauhaus collection. A continuum of art must exist in the museum,

to provide a firm basis for people to get a bearing in the future. It's true that a public gallery that specializes in temporary exhibitions can appeal more directly to the public, but not to the extent that it becomes an amusement hall, a place of entertainment. The private galleries are nothing whatever to do with the general public. The gallery owner's job is not to communicate things to a wide public but to 'keep the family informed'

JAPPE *The 'family' being those who spread the word in the art world?*

FISCHER Yes. I do an exhibition, it's seen by two people, they tell four others, they tell eight more - in six months there's a chain reaction. There is no art that is easily consumable. Warhol or Van Gogh make just as many demands on one as Conceptual Art; it's just that with paintings people think they've taken it all in in one look. I believe that art is understood only by professionals.

JAPPE *Aren't you inviting Left-wing accusations of élitism?*

FISCHER There is no such thing as an élite mentality except where the élite has control. This is just faulty reasoning on the part of the Left. Artists don't make art for an élite; they don't make it for anyone.

JAPPE *You mean they are governed by what Gottfried Benn called 'the compulsion to express'?*

FISCHER Better to call it a need, there's no compulsion. Art has no function; it's just art.

JAPPE *Art for Art's Sake, in other words.*

FISCHER Yes, that hasn't changed. The extension of consciousness can come about through any new object: the moon on television, for example. Any art that sets out to expand people's minds is nothing more nor less than education. Artists can't change society through their art, but through the influence they gain by means of their art. In spite of *Guernica*, Picasso was not a political artist. But if he were to say anything about politics now, it would get printed and people would read it. And the people who are interested in art are those that spontaneously get something out of it; they can be of any educational level, and they certainly don't belong to a class circumscribed by the IQ standards of the Establishment. Take artists like Barnett Newman or dealers like Schmela - they come from perfectly ordinary backgrounds.

JAPPE *And you don't want to give away anything definite about your future plans?*

FISCHER Yes, one thing. I am not going to need a gallery. I want to work as an art agent. What I want, and what my artists want, is to show my programme for a solid half-year somewhere where it hasn't been possible to see it before. I am thinking of London. My Düsseldorf and New York artists are known in the places where they live; but my London artists are better known in Düsseldorf and New York than they are in London.

Proposition for Reclaiming a Space

Bik Van der Pol

Proposal for a Collaboratorium on art and its Thought in the State Silk Museum, Tbilisi

Bureau For Progressive Bureaucracy

CONTENTS

* It is recommended that the reader first read the Appendix, 'A Brief History of the Silk Museum (Anonymous Document)', before starting chapters in this pamphlet.

75

CHAPTER 1: Collaboratorium

co-

1: with : together : joint : jointly <coexist> <coheir> 2: in or to the same degree <coextensive> 3a: one that is associated in an action with another : fellow : partner <coauthor> <coworker> b: having a usually lesser share in duty or responsibility : alternate : deputy <copilot> 4: of, relating to, or constituting the complement of an angle <cosine>

labour

1a: expenditure of physical or mental effort especially when difficult or compulsory. b(1): human activity that provides the goods or services in an economy. b(2): the services performed by workers for wages as distinguished from those rendered by entrepreneurs for profits b(3): the physical activities (as dilation of the cervix and contraction of the uterus) involved in giving birth; also: the period of such labor. 2: an act or process requiring labor. b(3): a product of labor. 4a: an economic group comprising those who do manual labour or work for wages. b(1): workers employed in an establishment. b(2): workers available for employment collaborate.

laboratory (laboratorium)

1: to work jointly with others or together especially in an intellectual endeavor 2: to cooperate with or willingly assist an enemy of one's country and especially an occupying force 3: to cooperate with an agency or instrumentality with which one is not immediately connected.

4: a place equipped for experimental study in a science or for testing and analysis; broadly : a place providing opportunity for experimentation, observation, or practice in a field of study b: a place like a laboratory for testing, experimentation, or practice <the laboratory of the mind>5: an academic period set aside for laboratory work.

collaboratorium

76

CHAPTER 2: Asymmetrical Rooms of Museum Practice

For a collaboratorium on art and its place in the State Silk Museum, careful observation of the museum's two main spaces is required. These two spaces are namely the display room where the museum's collection, together with a portrait gallery is exposed; and the former conference hall.

The display room (also referred to as exposition) is particularly interesting – in relation to the story of the display furniture saving the collection and the museum (see Appendix), but also in relation to modernity. The founding of the museum, together with the former production and research complex, is loaded with notions of progression, curing, production, knowledge, collecting (specimens) and classification – all notions immediately related to modernity.

The notion of progress, and maintaining that progress, which encapsulates the moment of Modernity together with its specimens, turns the whole exposition into a specimen, that remains in exactitude; hence becoming a complete opposite of its progressive initiation. The exposition itself becomes a cocoon, or a time capsule, that remains more than 100 years untouched.

Thus, there already exists a contrast between the two main rooms. The display room is treated as a time capsule and the former conference hall as a weightless vessel. As a space that can be filled and emptied easily, this vessel frequently relinquishes its load. In other words, an ever-changing/living/art/work space that is the collaboratorium.

CHAPTER 3: Certain Pre-Determined Activities
(or rather a lexicon on their physical expectancies)

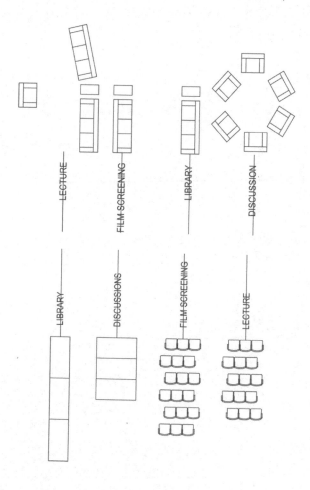

CHAPTER 4: Claiming Space (exemplary modes of territorial conquest)

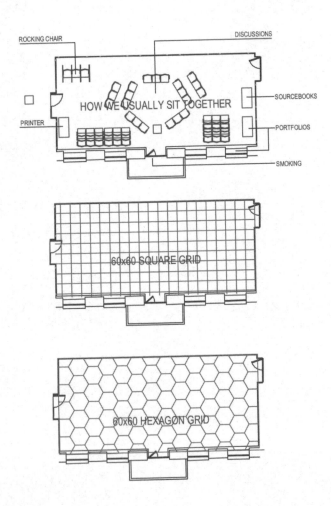

CHAPTER 5: Conclusion

One should not rely on preconceived modes of conduct, including those provided in this pamphlet. However, a contrast with the encapsulated display room, which is extremely preserved and static in all its glory, is still very much worth pursuing as an activity that takes place in the former conference hall.

Dwelling on what has been observed, there are several issues and things to abandon considering the space, such as the need to abandon dependency on other power-centers; abandoning the disciplinary boundaries of art and art history and exploring beyond these fields (not necessarily to believe, but to know) instead of the immediate eagerness to look geographically outside. Or, as hinted in the previous sentences, to abandon self-weakening positions, as in expecting international (Western) actors to define, help, teach, support, recognise, affirm and validate; further, as in taking on defeatism, bitterness and the constant expression of the lack. And finally to abandon local/regional and global provincialism, and all the things they bring.

In a sense, the former conference room should abandon what it clings to and what clings to it, to maintain the asymmetry between itself and the museum display (also referred to as exposition).

The definitions of function and production need to be questioned and rewritten constantly.

APPENDIX

The State Silk Museum: A Brief History
Date of establishment: 1887
Total space of the organisation: 395 m^2
Display space: 298 m^2
Storage space: 31 m^2
Quantity of stored items: 5,182
Budget status: Governmental
Legal status: Legal subject of public law (2006)
Under the governmental control of: Ministry of Culture, Sport and Monument Protection, Georgia
Partner organisations: Georgian Textile Group, European Textile Network, Budapest Textile Museum.

In 1885, 27-year-old Nikolas Shavrov was sent to Lyon by the Russian emperor to study the cocoon disease in France, Germany, Italy and Dual Empire. Inspired by the Lyon textile laboratory collection, he decided to build a museum.

The Caucasian Sericultural Station was founded in the Georgian capital Tbilisi in 1887. In 1892 the main facilities of the building were constructed on the premises of the underappreciated Mushtaidi garden. These included areas for administration, the library and exhibition hall. The Polish-born A Shinkevich was the building's architect. Then living in Tbilisi, Shinkevich worked under the rule and guidance of Shavrov, who, in 1909, was sent as an ambassador to Turkestan. The Caucasian Sericultural Station closed with all buildings remaining intact.

Before 1930 there was no staff working permanently in the building of the Caucasian Sericulture Center, which during that year became known as Undercaucasus Scientific Research Institute of Sericulture. These years, full of conferences, and travelling, are remembered as the best years by the members of the institute.

During the Second World War, the families of officers serving in the Soviet Army occupied the first floor of the building.

In 1954, the status of the institute was transferred from union level to the level of Georgian Soviet Socialist Republic.

In 1969, the staff of the museum moved to another building, and the exponents of the museum were totally forgotten.

In 1986, the museum was handed to Dynamo Stadium, originally established in 1933 and temporarily named Lavrenti Beria Stadium. After coming to the opening of the stadium and going through the museum, Beria decided to leave the museum untouched. But 53 years later the museum faced the risk of being turned into a hotel for stadium visitors. It was only the furniture – handmade and a unique example nineteenth-century craftsmanship – that saved the museum; a carpenter sent by the Dynamo Stadium to dismantle the building contents reported the furniture as impossible to reconstruct.

Following this, the job was left for a future date, which was never pursued, and the building was left totally derelict. At one stage, the roof collapsed.

In 1991, a campaign to support the museum was initiated by its director and a fellow art historian. Together with a photo album prepared by Shavrov in 1900, they visited several institutions and managed to gain the support necessary to renovate and open to the public for the first time in the museum's tumultuous history.

On 6 January 2006, the Silk Museum was registered as a museum and came under the protection of the Ministry of Culture, Sport and Monument Protection. In the same year the Stalin portrait, a lithograph on silk became part of the portrait gallery that overhangs the exposition. The mentioned portrait was found together with a Lenin lithograph on silk, which still remains in storage.

Now the Silk Museum has many friends, among them there are artists. Zurab Tsereteli, an honorary member of the museum, financed the trip to Moscow for two museum members to take part in the 140th anniversary of Shavrov. Geoair, a young art collective, organises events in the museum.

Based on the interview with Irina Tchotorlishvili.

Tbilisi, 2008.

Granville Cube

public works

The Cube is a simple metal frame structure that travels to various locations on and around the Granville New Homes site. The structure acts as a communication and facilitation device on-site. It hosts small-scale local events and collects and stages ideas for use in the public realm.

The cube features a weekly on-site programme that ranges from carol singing to swap shops and flower planting to mega fish tanks. Simple add-ons transform the cube into an exhibition space, small stage, outdoor screen or workshop space.

All events and works-in-progress are announced on the billboard. The cube will be appropriated over time and became an archive that enacts ideas for the public space.

The 'Granville Cube' constituted the third incarnation of the cube prototype. It is part of the public art programme that ran alongside the Granville New Homes Development, by Levitt Bernstein Architects in South Kilburn, between September 2005 and August 2007. Early incarnations of the cube resulted in an instant cube as for the Cut&Paste project, the Penbury Cube proposal (both with Nicoline van Harskamp) and the mobile bbcube.

bbcube

Cut & paste kitchen cube
Kathrin Böhm / Nicoline van Harskamp / Lisa Cheung

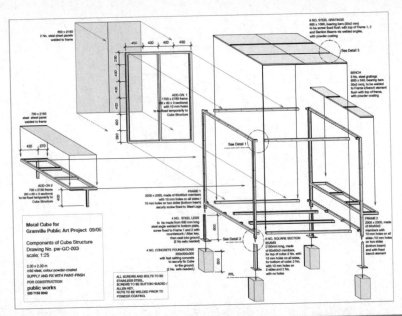

Granville cube

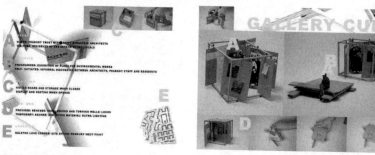

The Penbury cube
public works / Nicoline van Harskamp

Letterheads

Luis Camnitzer

In a society that presently is unwilling to grant me the power I deserve I have to create my own alternative power structure. As an artist I started this process several decades ago by collecting museums (I have more than thirty) to keep them from collecting me. I'm aware of the dangers of corruption; therefore, with criteria that satisfies social responsibility, I only create institutions I consider useful for the construction of a better society. And I try to avoid any abuse of power.

The Self-Proclamation Club (Luis Camnitzer, President)

The Committee for the Nationalisation of Government (Luis Camnitzer, President)

The Ecumenical Church for Ethical Cynicism (Luis Camnitzer, Founder and Spiritual Advisor)

Misanthropes Anonymous (Luis Camnitzer, President)

Prophets Without Borders (Luis Camnitzer, Possible President)

The Inhibited Sociopaths Society (Luis Camnitzer, President)

Unique Centre for the Fight for Absolute Unanimity (Luis Camnitzer, Supreme Coordinator)

EL CLUB DE LOS AUTOPROCLAMADOS Luis Camnitzer, Presidente

COMITÉ INTERNACIONAL PARA LA NACIONALIZACIÓN DE GOBIERNOS

Luis Camnitzer
Presidente

IGLESIA ECUMÉNICA DEL CINISMO ÉTICO

LUIS CAMNITZER, FUNDADOR Y ASESOR ESPIRITUAL

MISÁNTROPOS ANÓNIMOS

Luis Camnitzer, Presidente

PROFETAS SIN FRONTERAS
PROPHÈTES SANS FRONTIÈRES
PROPHETS WITHOUT BORDERS

Luis Camnitzer
Presidente Posible

SOCIEDAD DE SOCIÓPATAS INHIBIDOS

Luis Camnitzer
Presidente

Centro Único de Lucha por la Unanimidad Absoluta

Luis Camnitzer, Coordinador Supremo

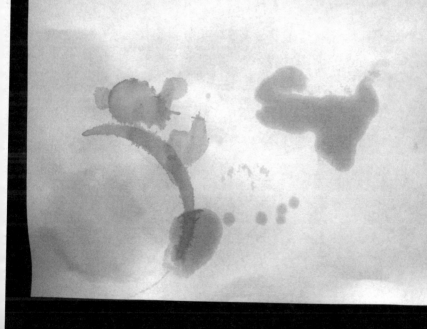

Thing 000913

(stock plan #77-870)

Agency

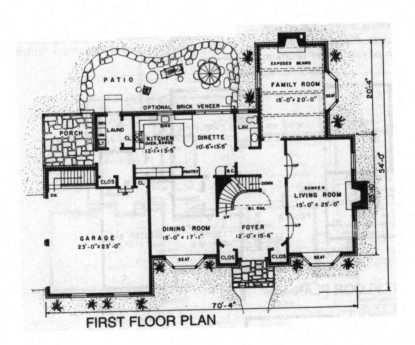

FIRST FLOOR PLAN

Thing 000913 (*stock plan # 77-870*)

In June 1977, Mr. and Mrs. Meltzer had ordered Robert Doran of the Xenco company to construct a four-bedroom residential home to be located in Livingstone, New Jersey. They chose an existing stock plan called *Chateau Gaye*. The plan was published in a plan book, called *101 Custom Homes*, made by the architect William Chirgotis. Xenco commissioned the architectural firm of William Chirgotis to prepare the plans. The Meltzers made thumbnail sketches indicating their desired changes. On 30 September 1977, Matthew Zito, an architect associated with William Chirgotis, finished an adapted plan according to the Meltzers's stated requirements. This plan was called *plan # 77-870*. Xenco received five copies of the plans for construction. He gave one to the Meltzer family.

In February 1979, a couple named Mr. and Mrs. Zoller contacted Robert Doran of the Xenco construction company concerning the construction of a home in Livingston, New Jersey. Together they visited a home that Xenco had finished before in the area for the family Meltzer. The Zoller family liked the house and decide to built one similar to it. Xenco commissioned Chirgotis to prepare the plans for the Zoller home. The Zollers chose the existing *stock plan # 77-870* used for Meltzer's home.

On 10 July 1979, after seeing the Zoller house, Meltzer filed a complaint in the Superior Court of New Jersey alleging copyright infringement of the *Meltzer plans*. Meltzer stated that the architectural plans of the home were commissioned works for hire of which he is the author. On August 17, 1981, the court case *Meltzer v. Zoller* took place at the United States District Court in New Jersey. Judge Whipple held that:

"[Meltzer] could not take advantage of the work for hire doctrine, since architectural plans do not fall within one of the statutorily prescribed categories of work. [...] Also Xeno commissioned the architectural plans for the Meltzer house. And they had an oral understanding that the architect keeps the rights to the plan. [...] Accordingly, any copyright interest which exists in the plans for the Meltzer home belongs to the Chirgotis architectural firm as preparers of the plans. [...] [Meltzer] prepared sketches illustrating in some detail features of the house which he and his wife required, and presented such sketches to the architect, Mr. Zito. It is also true that throughout the evolution of the plans, plaintiff contributed ideas and made certain changes and exercised approval power. But it cannot be gainsaid that the Chirgotis firm, as the architects, are the creators of the plans, and that the architectural firm designed plans and contributed most of the ideas contained therein. The home, a four-bedroom French colonial, is substantially similar to the Eastbrooke and the Chateau-Gaye, two plans designed by the Chirgotis firm and incorporated in the Chirgotis manual, 101 Custom Homes. [...] Mr. Zito testified that this type of consultation between client and architect, including the presentation of plans for other houses to the client, and coordination of the client's desires in the plans, is typical in the architectural profession, as well as standard practice at the Chirgotis firm. [...] Although Harvey Meltzer [...] contributed ideas and made certain changes and exercised approval power, it was the architectural firm which had created the plans for the house, and thus the architectural firm was author of plan for purpose of copyright interests. [...] Nor can Harvey Meltzer be considered a joint author of the plans. [...] [A] joint work is one prepared by two or more authors with the intention that their contributions be merged into inseparable or interdependent parts of a unitary whole. [...]"

The court concluded that Meltzer was not the author and also not the joint author of the architectural plan *stock plan # 77-870* and dismissed the action.

Hidden Curriculum

A project by Annette Krauss, held at
Casco, Utrecht, The Netherlands
17 September – 18 November 2007

Emily Pethick and Annette Krauss

Introduction

Hidden Curriculum looks at the unintended and unrecognised forms of
knowledge, values and beliefs that are part of learning processes and daily life
within high schools.

The 'hidden curriculum' can be seen to exist alongside every learning
process both inside and outside of school. Many students use tricks and tactics
to cope with the requirements they face within their education. They often
discover that their assigned schoolwork comes into conflict with their hobbies,
particularly in their spare time, and as a consequence selectively neglect
parts of the formal education. Often unnoticed, these activities constitute a
large part of the students' engagement during class yet go unrecognised as
forms of knowledge. Examples of this include a variety of cheating methods
and strategies that students develop in order to access their own interests
during their lessons, such as listening to music. 'Hidden Curriculum' focuses
on the kinds of actions that are developed by the students that go beyond
existing norms, showing creative ways of navigating institutional structures and
subverting enforced cultural values and attitudes.

The project will be realised through a series of workshops with two groups
of students (aged 15–16) from two schools in Utrecht. The workshops set
a framework in which the students investigate their own actions and forms of
behaviour and transfer the knowledge gained from their investigations towards
other ends, such as the production of printed material, video and public
actions. Activating situations that may go beyond common sense or secure
behaviour, they will reflect on the legitimacy of a specific social context, taking
a critical stance towards their own actions in order to act independently, think
creatively, and address the complexity of their own actions.

97

The workshops take place during school time in a variety of settings that include classrooms, the school building, Casco's space, and other sites within the city. These settings give the students varying degrees of publicness and privacy to deal with. The school environment is a highly coded environment, but also one that they are accustomed to and have established habits within. At the workshops held at Casco, the students are offered a more free and unfamiliar environment that establishes a distance to the school. Inherent in the project is a sense of inclusion and exclusion, visibility and invisibility. The students decide what can be accessed and what remains for a selected audience, ie out of reach of their teachers, parents and other figures of authority.

At Casco the students will work within a workspace developed specifically for the project by Céline Condorelli, as part of her ongoing research into support structures. Here the concept is to use existing structures and adapt them to their own use or benefit through subtle distortion or adjustemnt. The space is cloaked by a large set of curtains that spiral into the centre of the room, creating the possibility of two separate spaces, one more private and the other more open. The curtains can be assembled in layers of transparent and opaque material – ranging from coloured translucent plastic, to hessian and wool – and enable different levels of openness and privacy that allow the students to decide how public certain moments and parts of the project can be. The space is furnished with a set of tables and cupboards that are comprised of joined parts of existing furniture, which can be kept together or separated. These adaptable elements offer the students multiple possibilities to change their environment.

When venturing out into the city, the group will observe everyday life in the public sphere and will try and test it out by slightly changing the 'curriculum'. For example, what could the actual distances between people in public indicate? What happens if one changes one's own distance to other people? The challenge is to identify their own particular field research that can be tested.

Through looking at how the students negotiate and resist the formal structures that they are confronted with in the school environment, as well as transferring these investigations into the public realm, the project forms a model of how institutional structures are negotiated in other areas of life, observing how people deal with rules and internalise them, as well as subconsciously resist them. How do norms and values control our know-

how and practices in everyday life? How do these contribute towards the development of human relations within social contexts? What is the meaning of imposed categories of thought that are embedded in the very modes of particular actions?

Stages of Development

1. Collecting chairs

Each student was asked to donate a chair from their home as a way of demonstrating their commitment to the project and as a sign of their participation. The chairs are collected from their homes and assembled in the space at Casco, the invidual choices of the students created an odd array of different kinds of seating.

2. In the classroom – chair exercise

The students were asked to interact with a school chair in a way that goes against their usual uses of the object.

3. In the school – building exercise

The chair exercise is expanded in scale to encompass the building. The students set off to investigate the school building, finding ways to approach it that are different to the way in which they habitually navigate it. The students look for inbetween or non-spaces, seeking the gaps within the building that are not used, inconvenient, uncomfortable, forbidden and hidden spaces. They physically enter into them and document their findings.

4. Sharing tricks

What would the equivalent of these inbetween or non-spaces be as an action? The students are invited to reflect upon what they have done and relate that to their own actions. They are shown parts of an archive of interviews in which students from other schools share the secrets of their hidden actions. As many of these video clips were taken in Germany, the video sets off a discussion about differences in school structures, in particular between what is allowed or not within particular contexts. Even within the Netherlands, the differences between the two schools and their approaches to rules and structures are remarkable. This became visible in the discussions between the students. They contributed with video sequences towards the hidden curriculum archive.

5. Transferring into actions

The archive is taken as a starting point for a brainstorming session in which the students develop their own ideas of how to transfer these tricks into other actions. The intention of this is for the students to find their own particular field of interest that raises questions surrounding the broader topic of the investigation: the hidden curriculum.

6. Student-led research

Each student developed their own research project within the framework of the 'hidden curriculum.' These ranged from interviewing the school janitor to get his point of view, or setting up football training lessons in order to see how one could develop new tricks. Two students sat in on a test for a class in the year below them and observed the kinds of cheating methods the students were using.

7. Performative situations

The students found ways to intervene in the everyday processes of the school. Actions included switching around lockers, riding a bike through the different floors of the school and moving all of the plants in the building to block a corridor. Each created a way of altering the other students' and teachers' normal paths through the building, forcing them to negotiate something and temporarily change their habits.

8. Public actions

The students moved the investigation out into public space, looking at ways to counter the normal flows of the city, encountering the regulatory procedures within public space, and attempted to test it out by slightly changing the 'curriculum'. For example, what would happen if one waits for the bus standing upside down?

Untitled

Luca Frei

2007
Collage on paper

Good Model

5-47R
,5400,8400
,5493,8493
5U

Opening

— the only thing i can do

is to cut you up.

let go

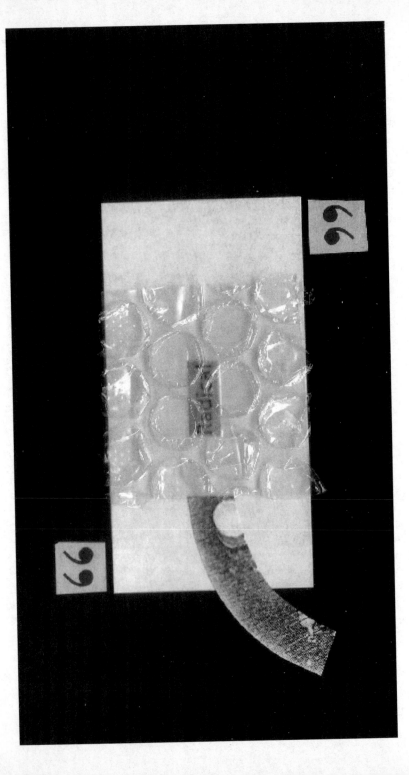

THEFT

Learning and Teaching

107

Forecasting

Broken Pasts

Becoming Globe
In Memoriam Hüseyin B Alptekin

Can Altay

Zone, Interzone, Setting:
William S Burroughs meets Timothy Leary on the way to J G Ballard

III

A Travelling Agency in Search of Sameness:

I won't even get into the hostility/hospitality phenomenon. The hotel signs that reveal pre-global fantasies, with names of places far and desired displayed in types dissociated, plexi-glass, always lit from within. The capacity for a place to become a city, through the act of naming. Hotel Bristol, one in every city, the yearning, a Monte Carlo all around the globe, remember the one in Minneapolis? When we really met each other for the first time. At least one Casablanca, in each and every city he travelled. On the other hand, Otel Arafat and Hotel Pele, just squeezed amongst the cities, the clue, of a person's capacity to become a place, a zone, embodying the interzone.

Days Past, Adventures Lost:

In an unknown apartment compartment in Havana. Grandmother shelling beans. Mother cooks while the daughter washes the dishes. A Beatles documentary plays on the TV, and we are sitting there on the couch. The son is out to get us cigars after rushing us in, out of sight. No longer walking near the factory across the street from where we are. The other night, Americanistas in the slums, rapping while driving us back in their small Yugo, pimped to the upmost watt possible, just like the pimp with the huge gold chain and rings. The phosphoric green Hawaiian shirt. The karaoke story with the untouchables in Tokyo, photojournalism in Africa, yearning for Zanzibar, shamanism in Mongolia, a teabag filled with stones and stuff, their incredible tea, kangaroo jerkies, and an old aboriginal lady playing the accordion to a song only she knows from where and which adventure. A seamless web. In an unknown room in Istanbul. Grandmother feeding the grandson, potato cooking on *tüpgaz* by the door, electric heater beside our feet. We are sitting there on the couch. The son, he has rushed us in, out of sight as we wait for outside to calm down. We saw guns in their hands.

113

Waiting for the Jetlag:

The quote from William Gibson, 'Souls can't move that quickly, and are left behind, and must be awaited, upon arrival, like lost luggage.' The jetlag, his global hangover, is as imperative as the in-flight tomato juice – a weak medicine against it. But lately I am happy that I got to meet with him. He joined a late lunch at Bambi and afterwards we went for coffee at Starbucks, 'at least its socialist in itself,' he said. We spoke for quite a long time. Not letting gossip take over, not rushing into some festivity. We talked about the global condition and how he was (he said we were) literally exercising what he (we) criticised in terms as global capitalism. All these philosophers and theorists, he said, the minor artists and curators, travelling all around, not thinking what it is, what it's all about. It is just something that strengthens the whole thing and distracts oneself with the act, he said. Or so I understood. He wasn't being fair on himself. Formally, perhaps, yes, it looked like it was the mere exercise of global mobility, as desired and produced by global capitalism, however, the reality he produced was of a different global field of responsibility and reflection, an aspatial utopia that made any border meaningless. It was this connectedness, that he called sameness.

114

Zoöpolis:

'The rats of Bombay solve the sewage problem of the whole city.' We see a giant insect, at a Milan Malpensa waiting-lounge café, with ice cream and the espresso. Speculations on which flight from which planet brought it here. The poor alien, scaring the workers who put him in a garbage bin, which is then carried out into the centre of the waiting lounge, lid open. Our flight is next, do insects have jetlag?

115

Notes and Knots:

Always in between *spins* and *yumaks*. Endless scriptures, within the notebook, which is then lost somewhere between Bilbao and Trintxerpe. An imperative element, an unrecoverable loss.

Depression and Delight:

'Once again the poem "Cidade" (Viva Vaia, Augusto de Campos, 1958) is
written with a thread of neon in Prozac green over a Viagra blue background.
The green shining through the lightness of blue with its one word that
leaves the effect of maybe being read or not, that is of two mental states –
depression and delight. A lampoon that has as much to do with this as with
miscomprehensions of conceptual art. In another corner of the exhibition sits
a diagnosis divan covered with a white cloth on which rest three white hoops
covered with white cloth, once again with the same light sources, expound
the three mottos of the exhibition. The white light "boredom"; the green
"loser"; and the blue "border".' (from an interview with Hüseyin B Alptekin
by Vasıf Kortun for Dulcinea catalogue, 1999. The first time I learn about
Alpekin's work).

Sounds and Letters. The Facts:

Forecasting a Broken Past. As with the Albanian bunkers, so with the equestrians, and with the quadriga. Or while following the trail of Jules Verne's *Kéraban-le-Têtu*. Taking a piece, bringing it around, fighting against history, or rather correcting it. Connecting it to presence in a way that it writes itself anew. Forecasting a broken past. Chasing broken histories. One object with a thousand stories and even more meanings. Dealing with monuments; monuments make one dis-remember. Chasing objects, chasing people, chasing people's objects. He brought together all the framed pictures in every household in a small town in western Australia, only to show in a space in that very town, to them, taking, giving back, and after the show, yeah, giving each back where they belong. Temporarily revealing. The constellation that is called community, with the rugby player portraits, the occasional oil on canvas quasi-Napoleonic equestrians, the falling water landscapes, aboriginal labourers, the ancestors, European portraits, the ancestors, a contemporary equestrian (photo from a contest), the cougar, the sheep of the year, a car without wheels, a car with wheels, more portraits, team portraits, sunflower field, ballerinas, thunder and lightning, Arnott's biscuits, workers' town, horses, carriage horses, work horses. The occasional furniture gathered from town, symmetrically placed in the room, same, but not identical. This was when I first thought about forecasting a broken past. Could have been a text on his work. Was going to be a text on his work.

On Becoming Globe:

He, who is also the biggest collector of globes I've seen. The revolving ones. In every possible size and material. Spread on the shelves of his library, and around his home. Reminiscent of his endeavour, one can become globe.

119

Full Moon and Eclipse:

Was always an issue, no? Came with an eclipse. Left at full moon.

Associative Dissociation or the Art of Displacement:

The good old tricks, for one last time. He's here and he's gone. Utopia that made any border meaningless. It was this connectedness, that he called sameness.

Commentary for
a Metatext

Peio Aguirre

Over the past few years I have written a number of essays in which I introduced some science fiction references. More precisely, the novels of William Gibson, one of the founders of the cyberpunk movement. These novels have made a pervasive influence on my thoughts concerning many diverse issues, such as consumption, identity, modernism, historicism, temporality, objecthood, the sprawl, novelty and the new, globalisaton or postmodernism.

I am persuaded that all those subjects appearing together within an art context can modify our understanding of the world as much as challenge our vision on art. It is also certain that these essays are not 'art writings' but rather, non-disciplinary explorative incursions into the realm of cultural criticism or the contemporary. However, even if the media in which the writing itself appears are institutional catalogues or serious semi-academic journals for art criticism, the essays seek (in their modesty) to transcend and push the genres further (in the same way that sci-fi itself is a self-reflexive genre that expands its own boundaries). Contemporary readers are experienced in a variety of sophisticated fields and pop cultural phenomena. They are my audience.

And as for cyberpunk, William Gibson's 2003 novel *Pattern Recognition* triggered a series of meditations about the experience of history as well as the dialectic of identity and difference in our habits towards consumption in late-capitalist societies. The plot of this novel is based in the present of post 9/11 and highlights a representational shift in traditional sci-fi and cyberpunk (which supposedly revolves around the future only to show in allegorical fashion that it deals in our current conjuncture).

This 'future is now' notion not only modified the sci-fi genre itself, but also helped map our current world. In order to map, representational tools are required. Historically the function of the genre itself has provided narrative structures that elaborate on cultural artefacts. If the genre of realism has been operative in the past to depict a reliable image of the world, the current complexity of our global condition seems to favour sci-fi as a genre more suited to the task. (An exception here might be the TV series *The Wire*, a truly realist genre from a historical perspective).

In the following contribution I highlight and de-contextualise excerpts from essays in which sci-fi references appear and rearrange them as fragments that comprise a new context. I am searching for new connections, new readers and new forms. Rather than writing a new fully autonomous text – similar to a collage in which borders are visible but an organic form is preserved – I have decided to emphasise its fragmentary condition as fully autonomous short texts. Therefore, the text from which they originate is, in a sense, made visible. However, I have maintained the original footnotes in succession to perpetuate the illusion of a conventional text.

Fragments on Cyberpunk

Peio Aguirre

William Gibson's novel *Pattern Recognition* is set in a recent past that seems to be tomorrow. The book revolves around the advent of new modes of consumption and the development of a hyper-educated sense of smell capable of identifying new patterns. In the book, Gibson weaves a paranoid plot of global conspiracy under the watchful clinical eye that re-examines the emergence of new models, styles and types of behaviour. In a pop-cultural context, the tendency is to recognise and detect the new, just as detectives use clues to guess the totality of a plot. Gibson invents the metaphor of the 'mirror-world' to describe the continual referentiality of the world in its scattering of names, brands and signatures. One of the ideas is that we live in a mirror-world, in which everything is the reflection of something else, something that is both identical and different. This mirror-world is sustained by the contradictory balance between the increased uniformity of lifestyles and the need for singularity, as if in this mirror-world a text has to be placed in front of a mirror so that it can be read, since in its original nature it remains cryptically back-to-front. Even though the world-as-text might function as a mirror that reflects society, it is always advisable to remain suspicious of mirrors because, as Lacan showed, they promote their own mode of false consciousness and above all they misinterpret. Cayce, the main character in Gibson's novel, describes London as a 'mirror-world' of the States in which everything looks alike and yet is different: 'A mirror-world in which we recognise ourselves but which is nevertheless sufficiently alien for us to think of it and read it with true fascination.'[1] A new version of the paired 'identity and difference' pivots around a form of consumer capitalism in which science fiction, or the description of a future imagined by the human brain, is no longer a vision of tomorrow but of yesterday. For Gibson, it is less a future than an alternative present.

There are few things that convey as much information to us as the advances in the image and in art and design. Exploring the 'mirror-world' phenomenon signifies developing a sensibility towards what Boris Groys identifies as the appearance of 'the new', the next thing to come. Groys writes that only when the conservation of the old seems to be assured by technology and civilisation, does an interest in the new arise; it is at this point that producing tautological or epigonic works begins to seem superfluous, as all they do is repeat what has already been in the archive for a long time. [2]

In the novel, the author of *Neuromancer* scrutinises a post-9/11 diagnosis stratified like a moment in which the referential complexity and the instantaneous ossification of culture predicts that 'One day we'll need archaeologists to help us guess the original storylines of even classic films.' [3] A contributing factor is Gibson's language that excludes all but insiders. This is a language based, to a certain extent, on name-dropping, the reduction of ideas and the images of things to their names. The complicity shared privately by the writer and the reader concerning this or that reference generates a cult of indicators and these selfsame references function as empty signifiers whose sole usefulness is that they are mere activators of desire and the unconscious.

Cayce's skill is that she can identify a pattern and then 'point a commodifier at it.' [4]

A soft analysis that goes from the superficial commentary to descriptive sophistication: 'Homo sapiens are about pattern recognition', he says. 'Both a gift and a trap.' [8]

This patterning system is one of the central aspects of postmodernity, the way in which all these objects no longer function as the expression of an individual subjectivity but instead participate in a broader movement of the cultural production of capitalism. This (postmodern) historicism has by no means disappeared; everyday, new cases emerge in the realm of consumer culture and the arts. The breaking of the bonds between the sign and its referents promises an infinite chain of texts (not all necessarily verbal) in which the external world shares in this illusion of the reference and in which the original is lost among an indeterminate layering of strata of every kind. Consequently, a literary text can also be treated as an artefact, as a piece of culture, differing only in degree from Mayan urns or Regency vases. Recognition

and reference go hand in hand, and the ultra-referentiality of culture is like a spectral shadow that phantasmagorises the past, enveloping it in the fog of vagueness and confusion.

Excerpt taken from the essay 'Notes on History, Periodization and Pattern Recognition', in the catalogue *Archaeologies of the Future*, sala rekalde, Bilbao, 2007.

The Novum and the Novelty of the Next-to-Last Thing

If the remains of pop culture act as historical forms of periodisation, the dialectic between the old and the new offers us a wide spectrum of possibilities for thinking about historical time. Etymologically, the new has been equivalent to the modern. The inquiry into the age of our modernity has produced antinomies that only lead to a linguistic cul-de-sac. A similar rhetoric surrounds the question of how our recent past exists. The exploration of the new reflects something that is always about to ensue or that is yet to be (new). Perhaps the truly new is the latest novelty after the latest novelty? Nonetheless, what is the nature of the current status of the latest thing? And what is the validity not of the latest thing, but of the one before it, the next-to-last novelty? In its ontology, the meaning of the 'next-to-last' is clarifying: 'the last thing before the last'.

Few titles befit a reflection on history as well as that one, of a work by Siegfried Kracauer, in which he wonders if ageing is simply conceiving the future as the future of the past, that is, history. [5] For Kracauer, philosophy is concerned with the last things, whereas history attempts to explain 'the last thing before the last.' He writes, 'once a vision becomes an institution, clouds of dust gather about it, blurring its contours and content. The history of ideas is a history of misunderstandings.' [6] We could draw a parallel line between this tracking of the next-to-last things – as opposed to the vacuity and lightness of new design objects, useless artefacts and idioms derived from advertising in its immediate process of absorption, assimilation and forgetting – and the ability of cultural theory and the historian-scientist-curator not to find new things, but to rediscover the old as the most recent novelty available for semiotic and ideological dissection. History here is the object of a thorough reinvention, as if everything that had previously been delivered to us from the past were just a bad joke in need of correcting or, perhaps, re-rendering current. A theory of the next-to-last things, and not of the last things, accentuates the recent past and the near future; nonetheless, the utopian nature of temporal concepts, such as the 'day before yesterday' and 'the day after tomorrow', remains intact while encouraging a pop-like appropriation in which the past-present-future sandwich is the object of temporal mediation (an intrinsically pop gesture).

Dialectically, this consideration of the utopian potential of the next-to-last thing is useless without its inevitable reversal and antidote; that is, everything that is yet to be or is to come. Ernst Bloch is credited with a way of proceeding that aspires to see thinking geared towards the future not as an extension of the present, but as open to the novum, to the not-yet-conscious, and its objective correlate, that which has-not-yet-come-into-being. The latency of the not yet is correlative to the novum, the new or that reality that has yet to be. The novum is not a new piece inserted in a mundane and essentially unalterable environment, but rather a new reality that has never existed, one that aims to wholly reconstruct the world around it, creating, de facto, a new world, a new reality, where the not-yet-conscious can take place, enter history and transform it. Both the theory of science fiction and revolutionary consciousness can benefit from this. [7] This not-yet-of-the-utopian imagination contrasts with the 'already ensued' typical of conservative positions that time and again have sounded the monotonous drone of the end of history. That which has not yet been, or is about to be 'the hope principle' and the next-to-last things shape a horizon of the utopian imagination worth furthering.

Excerpt taken from the essay 'For a Theory of the Next-to-Last Things', in the catalogue *Before Everything*, CA2M, Centro Dos de Mayo, Mostoles, Madrid, 2010.

The book: In *Pattern Recognition*, William Gibson describes a world in which everything is a reflection of something else. One of the stylistic features of Gibson's previous novels, such as *Neuromancer*, is their minute description of objects and situations not strictly bound to any particular period, but which the reader presumes to belong to some indeterminate (science-fiction) future. Here, however, he offers a futuristic X-ray of the present, setting the story in the recent past, specifically in the days following 9/11.

The plot: Gibson uses the metaphor of this 'mirror-world' to examine the progressive aestheticisation of the world and the consequent deference to the laws of the market, with its perpetual novelties and increasingly sophisticated products being decoded by 'coolhunters', searching for the latest trend or emerging brand. The central character, Cayce Polar, has from her earliest childhood developed an innate ability to recognise shapes and patterns, to

identify forms of behaviour in a kind of semiology of everyday detail closely related to the nascent discipline of archaeology.

However this gift for design has its own unwelcome side-effects; Cayce is hypersensitive to brands; she suffers from a kind of agoraphobia towards logos and designs, and the black hole of her affection – the ground zero from which a whole paranoid pathology begins to take her over – is Bibendum (the Michelin Man). The only antidote is to erase all the distinctive style marks of a product, followed up by compensatory therapy that avoids brand-consumption through an itemised metacommentary on everything. In practical terms, this means getting rid of any trace of evident style, and searching for some Barthesian generic or 'white label' equivalent, for Cayce 'is, literally, allergic to fashion. She can only tolerate things that could have been worn, to a general lack of comment, during any year between 1945 and 2000. She's a design-free zone, a one-woman school of anti whose very austerity periodically threatens to spawn its own cult. [8]

Identification kicks in when the desire to repeat a norm, a guideline or a pattern, reaches the point of reproduction; people are paid to work as freelance promoters, dropping into wine bars to chat up and let slip the names of some as-yet non-existent products.

Style: The 'mirror-world' is, to a certain extent, a metaphor for the degree of sophistication which products in our time have taken. Behind it all is not so much the exhaustibility of creative talent for design but quite the opposite – the progressive stylisation of all worlds of life, a situation Hal Foster warned of in *Design and Crime*. [9] This 'mirror-world' is a place where identity and difference are inextricably tied up in a succession of never-ending mirror images.

The capacity to create a metacommentary on singular objects – an exhaustive analysis of the successive stylistic and formal layers of a trend – lies in the exclusivist use of references and in having them operate as cultural markers.

To this extent, despite its prolific use as a concept, in *Pattern Recognition*, style is a difficult category to grasp. Like the more visible face of an object, style becomes the key element for recognition, the vehicle for identification; yet 'style' is one of the most evasive, slippery and ambiguous concepts ever invented as a way of defining and distinguishing between different works, authors, periods, epochs and so on. First, style was a specifically modern or modernist phenomenon. The idea of inventing a personal non-transferrable style was linked to an entire construction of the individual subject of modernism. Thanks to style, we recognise ourselves in objects, in their design, and we symbolically come into contact with a whole community of consumers. Marcel Proust offered one of the most famous definitions when he said that having style consists of turning a foreign language into one of our own languages: literally, cannibalising. Digesting it and turning it into part of oneself. And it is has become a standard meal for artists and designers believing in recombination and appropriation (a thousand times over) of the aesthetics of the past.

'One day we'll need archaeologists to help us guess the original storylines of even classic films,' says one of the voices in *Pattern Recognition* before launching into a digression on the diminished value of the original in culture: 'Musicians, today, if they're clever, put new compositions out on the web, like pies set to cool on a window ledge, and wait for other people to anonymously rework them. Ten will be all wrong, but the eleventh may be genius. And free. It's as though the creative process is no longer contained within an individual skull, if indeed it ever was. Everything, today, is to some extent the reflection of something else.'[10] The best way of describing this 'mirror world' is as an archaeology of the future.

Excerpt taken from the essay 'Future Imperfect: from Canibalisation to Ex-design', in the catalogue *Destroy Design*, FRAC Nord Pas de Calais, Dunkerque.

For example, a study such as *Science Fiction and Critical Theory* by Carl Freedman seeks to develop the argument of the privileged genre within traditional Marxism and historical fiction, through what he sees as its natural successor: science fiction [11] – a type of popular literature that has a strong affinity with dialectic thought, and which in a way, has established itself as a minority genre whose centrality resides in a renewal of a dialectic vision of history.[12]

...

We have seen two aesthetic theories within the Marxist tradition: that of realism and that which is referred to as 'aesthetic form'. The insufficiency of each one requires us to take a stance that does not involve choosing one or the other; nor does it mean dialectically choosing the two by combining them. While it would be no unhealthy exercise to identify artistic practices (or artists) that embrace all these trends and discourses at the same time, the stumbling blocks of realism today lie in the impossibility of capturing the real without engaging a million filters; and something similar happens with

the invention of a new form that is not in itself indebted to other older ones. When more than realism, we have reflections on realism, and the same happens with the formal, the challenge is to open gaps in the hyper-coding of culture or, on the contrary, to saturate the referentiality and the meta-commentary of the work in such a way that it becomes a sort of cognitive map of the absent totality.

Projecting a future form of art that does not (yet) exist is quite a task for the imagination; a form of art that contains the main features of a highly coded world, where everything revolves around branding, the marketing of styles, the over-laden and designed novelty, immaterial labour and the semiotics of the environment. Art resembles those other areas where the manufactured world is not as important as the marketing of goods and the management of information. Of course, objects, books and films continue to be produced in important quantities. How should one imagine this future form of art?

In literature, to cite an example, the 'new realist novel' has consumed and filtered these hyper-coded mechanisms and has returned them as an art in the novels of William Gibson, and his invention of strange ambiguous forms such as 'footage', 'locative art', the 'semiotic ghosts', 'avant-garde marketing' and the exploration of 'negative space'. [13]

Excerpt from the essay 'Form, Meaning and Reality', in the reader *To the Arts, Citizens!* Fundaçao Serralves, Porto, 2010.

In William Gibson's 1981 short story 'The Gernsback Continuum', a photographer (the narrator) is commissioned to illustrate a coffee-table book about North American architecture of the 1930s, which will be published under the suggestive title *The Airstream Futuropolis: The Tomorrow That Never Was.* [14] Excavating the architecture of the so-called 'American Streamlined Moderne', full of chrome surfaces and buildings inspired by Fritz Lang's 1927 *Metropolis*, the narrator is haunted by what he calls the 'semiotic ghost': hallucinations of unrealised futures – an airplane that was 'all wing, like a fat symmetrical boomerang with windows in unlikely places' or 'fifth-run movie houses like the temples of a lost sect that worshipped blue mirrors and geometry.'[15] Gibson used this concept to describe the science-fiction imagery that permeates Western culture – that is, 'bits of deep cultural imagery that have split off and taken on a life of their own,' or to put it in another way, popular delusions about past culture. More precisely, Gibson's somewhat satirical criticism drew both on various modernist movements (which he labelled 'futuroids') and on the 1920s-esque fake pulp technology featured in sci-fi magazines such as Hugo Gernsback's *Amazing Stories*. Gibson's version of a futuristic pop ghost echoes that 'old-fashioned future' that Bruce Sterling, Gibson's cyberpunk peer, coined in the title of one of his books to describe the time-space shifts that tend to present the past as science fiction and science fiction as past. [16] 'The Gernsback Continuum' as a hilarious compilation of sci-fi tropes, also managed to short-circuit the categories historically assigned to the genre, and functioned instead as a critique of its own aesthetic clichés. It is for this and other reasons that this story is seen as inaugurating the cyberpunk sub-genre, which mixes sci-fi literature with postmodernism. [17]

But today Gibson's semiotic ghosts have transcended the realm of the science-fiction genre to shape our current cultural reception and our understanding of history. Gibson's account is one of the most valuable examples of a postmodern conception of history, particularly in postmodernism's challenging of social and political institutions, ideas of continuity and structure, the nature of historical research and knowledge. Today, much looks as if it were the product of a ceaseless proliferation of textuality, which holds that history never comes to us 'as it was', but in the form of texts and other documentary objects. Having now discarded the ideal that objective and factual knowledge of a historical reality is apprehensible, the past becomes a masterfully crafted text composed by infinite other texts up for refutation.

Excerpt taken from the essay 'Semiotic Ghosts: Science Fiction and Historicism', in *Afterall Journal* No 28 London, 2011.

This aside, postmodern hyperspace also found its natural field of expression in cyberpunk (the genre that mixes science fiction with postmodernism). This is where William Gibson came up with the concept of 'cyberspace', specifically in his 1984 novel *Neuromancer*. [18] In another prescient gesture, Gibson foresaw the connotations and significance that cyberspace would have in the Internet age, with an aesthetic that openly tracked the course of technological saturation as an extension of the human (including post-human prostheses). In his books, a black nylon flight jacket or the oscillating rhythm of a kinetic neon light in the dark room of a night club could synthesise the ellipse of a world symbolised by the move from an analogue to a digital culture, where the new hero (of postmodern narrative) is the urban punk, the cybernetic cowboy, the computer pirate and any other variant of freelance subjectivity. This distinction between the analogue and digital also encompassed money, with the shift from the logic of real (or

cumulative) capital, to what became known as financial, or speculative capital. [19] The spectral nature of capital is equivalent to worldwide phantasmagoria. In another innovative essay, Jameson remembers the cybernetic revolution: 'The intensification of communications technology to the point at which capital transfers today abolishes space and time and can be virtually instantaneously effectuated from one national zone to another,' adding, 'the results of these lightning-like movements of immense quantities of money around the globe are incalculable.'[20] In keeping with this, it is interesting to compare all the aesthetic variants that flourish in culture alongside the inrush of this type of capital. What underlies or originates so-called financial capital is simply 'a play of monetary entities which needs neither production (as capital does) nor consumption (as money does): which supremely, like cyberspace, can live on its own internal metabolism and circulate without any reference to an older type of content.' [21]

Moreover, what 1982's *Blade Runner*-style postmodernism more specifically showed us was the advent of the present in different guises of futurity (as in cyberpunk), and a nostalgia rooted in the inability to think about the future. Narrative scripts (or rather, scenarios) set in a near future served as allegories, while the condensation of culture – formalised in a Baroque style – reflected the crisis of historicity that I referred to earlier. *Blade Runner* condensed urban dystopia and the threat of overpopulation in a single blow, which partly explains all these seasoned references to Japanese culture spread throughout the globe, in one of the most authentic signs of the cyberpunk genre.[22]

Excerpt taken from the essay 'Lost in Space: From Hyperspace to Cognitive Mapping', in the catalogue *Passages: Travels in Hiperspace* LABoral, Gijón, T21 Thyssen-Bornemisza Art Contemporary, Vienna, 2010.

Endnotes
1. Back cover of the Spanish edition of *Pattern Recognition*, William Gibson, Mundo espejo (trans) (Madrid: Minotauro, 2004).
2. Boris Groys, Über das Neue. Versuch einer Kulturökonomie On the New. Essay on Cultural Economy (Munich, 1992).
3. Gibson, *Pattern Recognition*, (G P Putnam's Sons, 2003) p 68.
4. Fredric Jameson, 'Fear and Loathing in Globalization', *New Left Review*, vol 23 (London: 2003), p 112. Republished in the volume *Archaeologies of the Future: The Desire Called Utopia and Other Science Fictions* (New York, London: Verso, 2005) pp 384–392.
5. Siegfried Kracauer, *History: The Last Things Before the Last* (Princeton: Markus Wiener Publishers, 1995).
6. *Ibid*, p 7.

131

7. See Mark Bound and China Miéville (eds), *Red Planets: Marxism and Science Fiction* (London, Pluto Press, 2009).

8. William Gibson, *Pattern Recognition* (New York: Berkley Books) p 8.

9. Hal Foster, *Design and Crime (and Other Diatribes)* (New York, London: Verso: 2002).

10. Gibson. Op cit. p 75.

11. Carl Freedman, *Critical Theory and Science Fiction* (Middletown: Wesleyan University Press, 2000).

12. This thesis of Freedman's owes much to Fredric Jameson, who in his 1982 essay 'Progress versus Utopia' said that science fiction should be seen as the successor to the historical novel, the former emerging with Jules Verne around 1860, when the latter was losing its vitality and declining into the (naturalist) virtuosities of Flaubert's *Salammbô*. See Fredric Jameson, 'Progress versus Utopia, or, Can We Imagine the Future?', compiled in *Archaeologies of the Future, The Desire Called Utopia and Other Science Fictions* (London, New York: Verso, 2005).

13. William Gibson in the trilogy *Pattern Recognition* (2003), *Spook Country* (2007) and *Zero History* (2010), in which he appears to invent a genre of his own, which is no longer cyberpunk but rather something that lies between a treatise on aesthetics, design theory and industrial espionage.

14. William Gibson, 'The Gernsback Continuum', in the compilation *Burning Chrome* (New York: Arbor House, 1986). The title of the story refers to Hugo Gernsback (1884–1967), science fiction pioneer and creator of the first magazine of the genre, *Amazing Stories*, in 1926. The short story was also published in Bruce Sterling (ed), *Mirrorshades: The Cyberpunk Anthology* (New York: Arbor House, 1986).

15. *Ibid*, p 27.

16. See Bruce Sterling, *A Good Old-Fashioned Future* (New York: Bantam Spectra, 1999).

17. Additionally, William Gibson, in his 'Sprawl series', lays the ground for a use of technology that is new but at the same time happening in an unspecified future, one intimately connected to our modern condition. The 'Sprawl series' includes the trilogy of *Neuromancer* (New York: Ace Books, 1984), *Count Zero* (London: Victor Gollancz Ltd, 1986) and *Monalisa Overdrive* (London: Victor Gollancz Ltd, 1988), as well as the compilation of short stories *Burning Chrome* (1986).

18. William Gibson, *Neuromancer* (New York: Ace Books, 1984).

19. See Fredric Jameson, 'Culture and Financial Capital,' in *The Cultural Turn* op cit., 136–161.

20. *Ibid*, p 143.

21. *Ibid*, p 161.

22. For a description of *Blade Runner* within the cyberpunk poetic, see Jameson's analysis of the film within the narrative coordinates of dirty realism and the naturalism of late nineteenth-century bourgeois literature, with its wretchedness (what the French called *misérabilism*), the underworld and so on. Fredric Jameson, 'The Restrictions of Postmodernity' in *The Seeds of Time* (Columbia University Press, 1994).

High Rise

Chris Fite-Wassilak

Shields eyes from the glare, imagines instead a temporary vertical structure. Maybe a precarious high rise of sorts, where each floor is a single apartment, and as eyes scroll down each is a year:

1934: Designer, essayist and art critic Edoardo Persico (invited in 1929 to live in Milan by Pietro-Maria Bardi, to run his magazine *Belvedere*. He dies in 1936, three months before his Room of Honour at the sixth Milan Triennale opens to be renamed triumphantly the Room of Victory) and artist, architect and designer Marcello Nizzoli (a former Futurist, after the Second World War, he is an industrial designer for Olivetti, designing products such as the Lettera 22 typewriter) design a set of light metal grids to be used to display a series of photographs and documents; one such display for the Hall of the Gold Medals of the Exhibition of Italian Aviation, another for the annual electoral exhibition within the eighteenth-century vaulted hall of the Galleria Vittorio Emanuele.

1969: Kurt Vonnegut Jr (his first novel is printed as *Utopia 14* in 1954 and released under the enduring name *Player Piano* in 1966. He attempts suicide in 1984 and dies from complications after falling down a set of stairs in 2007.) releases what was intended to be his first novel, describing an alien race. His character Billy Pilgrim writes, 'All moments, past, present and future, always have existed, always will exist. The Tralfamadorians can look at all the different moments just that way we can look at a stretch of the Rocky Mountains, for instance. They can see how permanent all the moments are, and they can look at any moment that interests them. It is just an illusion we have here on Earth that one moment follows another one, like beads on a string, and that once a moment is gone it is gone forever.'

1978: Christopher D'Arcangelo (In 1975 he chains himself to the front door of the Whitney Museum. He commits suicide in 1979.) and Peter Nadin

133

(In 1962 he paints a wall white in Bromborough, and in 2011 he poses for a photograph where he holds two piglets on his farm in the Catskills) begin a gallery in Nadin's loft studio. An eight-month project gathered under the heading, 'The work shown in this space is a response to the existing conditions and/or work previously shown within this space,' they are attempting to make communal work by asking artists to cumulatively produce and display in the room. After showing the empty room with the title '30 Days Work', Daniel Buren adds a series of marks around the room's perimeter. This is followed with responses by Jane Reynolds, Peter Fend, and Rhys Chatham. Following D'Arcangelo's death, the names of Nadin, Lawrence Weiner (It's 2005, and he's saying, 'It's all about the content, and in fact it has less to do about the content than anyone would like to admit.'), Dan Graham and Louise Lawler are stenciled on the floor.

1967: Architect Michael Scott and art critic and former Guggenheim Museum director James Johnson Sweeney (1971 they are walking together along a windy coastline, making conversation as they are filmed from 4m away) begin the first of a series of exhibitions under the name Rosc (which derives from the Irish for 'eye' or 'vision' and 'battle-cry') that showcase contemporary artworks alongside ancient artefacts in Ireland. The exhibition is to take place every four years, featuring 50 living artists selected by a panel of international experts brought to an island largely unexposed to international artworks. Held within the draped hall of the Royal Dublin Society, artist and architect Patrick Scott hangs the paintings from wires suspended from the ceiling.

1987: Midway through writing his mini-series of comic books *The Watchmen* with illustrator Dave Gibbons, Alan Moore (In 1992 he writes the lines, 'The one place gods inarguably exist is in our minds where they are real beyond all refute, in all their grandeur and monstrosity,' which leads him to pronounce himself a magician in 1993. In 2012, he writes on the BBC about his satisfaction that his 1982 use of the Guy Fawkes mask was adopted by the hackers Anonymous) is writing a page with a nine-frame grid in which his character, Dr Manhattan, is sitting on Mars, looking at a photograph and counting down the seconds to when he will drop the photo on the ground. In 1985, he is holding the picture, not recognising himself in the photo from 1959, while recalling its details, a crystallised moment from the Palisades Amusement Park in New Jersey. He drops the photo and walks off to look at space, saying, 'All we ever see of stars are their old photographs.'

134

1968: Lina Bo Bardi (In 1947, as curator of a private museum housed within Brazil's Associated Press offices, she is hanging paintings from metal bars that run from floor to ceiling, and writes, 'no distinction is made between an old or a modern work of art.' In 2011, several replicas of her display panels are used, 11 in a temporary exhibition at Eindhoven's Van Abbemuseum, two as separators between MASP's kitchen and restaurant checkout line.) opens her Museum of Art Sao Paulo. Her open-plan floors are filled with controversial 'panel-easel' display panels – rectangles of glass propped up by cubes of concrete. Each sheet of glass holds a painting, arranged at the same height irrespective of chronology or typology, with the name of the artist, title of the work, and occasionally additional information on the reverse of the panel.

bring in the idea of spatial depth infused with time. The porous layers in space indicate the simultaneity of presence where [the] body moves through depth in time. That is when the body experiences the event of time and space in its continuity. The spatial porosity is a method for destabilizing the outlines and limits while displacing them back and forth in-between spaces. This continual closing and opening of space provides a room for the body to discover its own visibility among the invisibles created by the empty voids. Thus, the porosity in space will appear as a result of an uninterrupted flow of interpenetrated events within the spatial depth.[43]

"Well, we think that time 'passes', flows past us; but what if it is we who move forward, from past to future, always discovering the new? It would be a little like reading a book, you see. The book is all there, all at once, between its covers. But if you want to read the story and understand it, you must begin with the first page, and go forward, always in order. So the universe would be a very great book, and we would be very small readers."

"But the *fact* is," said Dearri, "that we experience the universe as a succession, a flow. In which case, what's the use of this theory of how on some higher plane it may be all eternally coexistent. Fun for you theorists, maybe, but it has no practical application—no relevance to real life. Unless it means we can build a time machine!" he added with a kind of hard, false joviality.

"But we don't experience the universe only successively," Shevek said. "Do you never dream, Mr Dearri?" He was proud of himself for having, for once, remembered to call someone "Mr".

2010: Shima Mohajeri, 'The Time of Place in Architecture: The Simultaneity of Spatial Depth and Steven Holl's Design Method', paper delivered at International Merleau-Ponty Circle Conference, Mississippi State University; September 2009, quoted in Gabriela Campagnol and Stephen Caffey, 'Pepper the Walls with Bulletts: Lina Bo Bardi's Museu de Arte de São Paulo', paper delivered at the Creating_Making Forum, University of Oklahoma, p 149.

1974: Ursula Le Guin, The Dispossessed, London: Gollancz, p 184.

1895–1974

Two Fragments of the Portuguese Colonial Past

Daniel Barroca

In 1895, to the south of what is known today as Mozambique, the last emperor of the African Empire of Gaza was captured. He was known in Europe by the name of Gungunhana, the Lion of Gaza. Under the command of Mouzinho de Albuquerque, he was captured in the fortified village of Chaimite by the Portuguese troops of King Carlos. After 397 years of permanence along the coasts of this territory, the Portuguese wished to make a show of power to the rest of the European colonial potencies, especially because some had revealed interest towards these territories after both the British Ultimatum and the Treaty of Berlin. In this particular episode of Portuguese colonial history, Ngungunhane was actually betrayed by the Portuguese, with whom he had always had cordial trade relations and even, at some point, considered to be his allies. He was deported to Portugal, where he was humiliated and insulted by throngs of Lisbon residents. Locked up as a criminal and set apart from his seven wives by the overt pressure of Catholic groups, he would be moved later to Angra do Heroísmo, in the Azores archipelago, where he would die in 1906. In 1953, Jorge Brum do Canto directed a movie, 'Chaimite', in which this same story is reported according to the rules instituted by the propaganda cabinet of the dictatorship then ruling Portugal.

In 1961, 55 years after the death of Gungunhana, with the Portuguese still holding sway over the territory, and the country under the iron fist of António de Oliveira Salazar's regime [1] , the Portuguese Colonial War commenced. This war would last for 13 years, leaving 8,200 dead and indelible marks on the people that participated: still today, not all are able to openly discuss it. In 1974, 79 years after the demise of Gungunhana's Empire and 555 years after the conquest of Ceuta and the first maritime travels along the Atlantic African coast, a military coup-d'état called the Carnation Revolution, put an end to the Portuguese empire.

Gungunhana's arrival to Lisbon, March 1896.
Homage to the dead soldiers in the African Campaigns, 1896

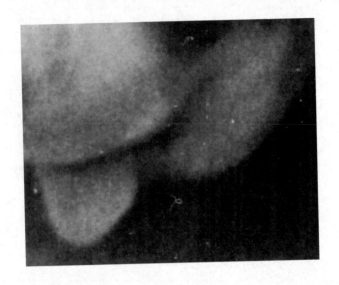

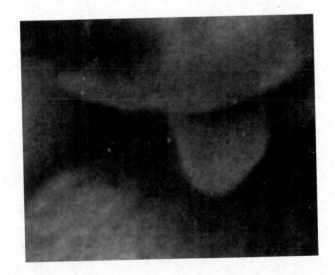

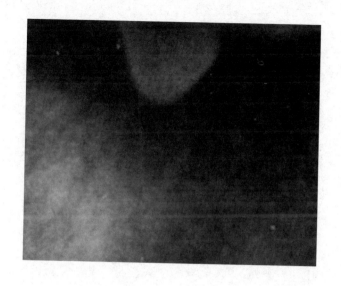

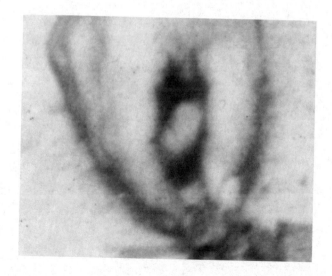

Text Translated by Pedro Moura from Portuguese
Image 1: Arquivo Municipal de Lisboa, José Chaves Cruz, CRU000195
Image 2: Arquivo Municipal de Lisboa, José Chaves Cruz, CRU000287
Film stills from 'Soldier Playing with Lizard,' created in 2008 at the residency program of the
Künstlerhaus Bethanien (Berlin) with the support of the Gulbenkian Foundation (Lisbon).

143

Endnotes

1. António de Oliveira Salazar was the founder of the fascistic and ultra-Catholic regime that ruled Portugal from 1926–1974. The regime was known as Estado Novo (New State) or Salazarism. Although Salazar died in 1969, the dictatorship continued, led by Marcelo Caetano, until the 1974 revolution.

The Frank Church – River of No Return Wilderness

Jeremiah Day

'Like Caesar peering into the colonies from distant Rome, Nixon said the choice of government by the Chileans was unacceptable to the president of the United States. The attitude in the White House seemed to be, "If in the wake of Vietnam I can no longer send in the Marines, then I will send in the CIA."'
– Frank Church, 1975

The absent knowledge of our recent past forms an inverted history and landscape in which secrecy, amnesia and ignorance form a generalised condition; where dug-up facts accumulate to form rare markers with which to guide ourselves.

'Freedom of opinion is a farce unless factual information is guaranteed and the facts themselves are not in dispute,' Hannah Arendt once remarked, and so the deposits of things not disclosed, events unknown deprive us not just of a past, but also a present (Can anyone today say with confidence whether or not any particular communication is being monitored, and to what degree?). 'Cover-ups' build in layers; conflicting false stories shape fake debates and discussions. The 'intelligence community' logs data and figures and even synthesises details into narratives. This community, however, remains isolated from each other and from any context, ultimately remaining hidden from the public where they might present or even become 'facts' or shared truths.

In previous times, there were secrets – holes in the public record – but now the publicly documented and understood event is the exception, the interruption.

For example, almost the entire body of knowledge of the secret services of the United States depends upon one exceptional investigation: The

145

United States Senate Select Committee to Study Governmental Operations with Respect to Intelligence Activities, widely known simply as the 'Church Committee', after the politician who led it.

CIA collaborations with the mafia in assassination attempts on Castro, the opening of international mail and telegrams (dating back to 1948) and the efforts to harass Martin Luther King Jr into killing himself in shame over his extra-marital lover are just the most picturesque episodes that punctuate the Church report. Domestically, the paperwork details the efforts of the police apparatus to infiltrate and disrupt the anti-war and civil rights movements, and in the most extreme case of the Black Panther leader Fred Hampton, murder dissidents. Outside the United States, Church said that 'covert actions' were simply a semantic disguise for murder, coercion, blackmail, bribery, the spreading of lies, whatever is deemed useful to bending other countries to our will.'

Frank Church, Senator from the rural mountain state of Idaho (1957–1981), was often mocked for his moralism; his colleagues called him Senator Sunday School. But can moralism explain this kind of practice of truth-seeking and truth-telling? And later, what propelled Church to travel across the United States, run for President in 1976 (winning several states in the primaries), speak of fundamental civic and republican principles such as the importance of means and ends. He said: 'American foreign policy must be made to conform once more to our historic ideals, the same fundamental belief in freedom and popular government that once made us a beacon of hope for the downtrodden and oppressed throughout the world.'

What is the interior landscape from which such public statements emerge? If almost everything we have available to us on this critical subject emerged from the maintenance and application of principle, led by an individual politician, does that not force a re-assesment of principle as a political power?

Church was also active in conserving the wilderness, and on his deathbed, an area of Idaho was named for him, as well as the famous river contained there. One can only wonder if anyone at the time had in mind the following quote made by Church about the surveillance techniques developed by the National Security Administration (the scope of which has only grown to this day):

'If this government ever became a tyranny, if a dictator ever took charge in this country, the technological capacity that the intelligence community has given the government could enable it to impose total tyranny, and there would be no way to fight back, because the most careful effort to combine together in

resistance to the government, no matter how privately it was done, is within the reach of the government to know. Such is the capability of this technology…

I don't want to see this country ever go across the bridge. I know the capacity that is there to make tyranny total in America, and we must see to it that this agency and all agencies that possess this technology operate within the law and under proper supervision, so that we never cross over that abyss. That is the abyss from which there is no return.'

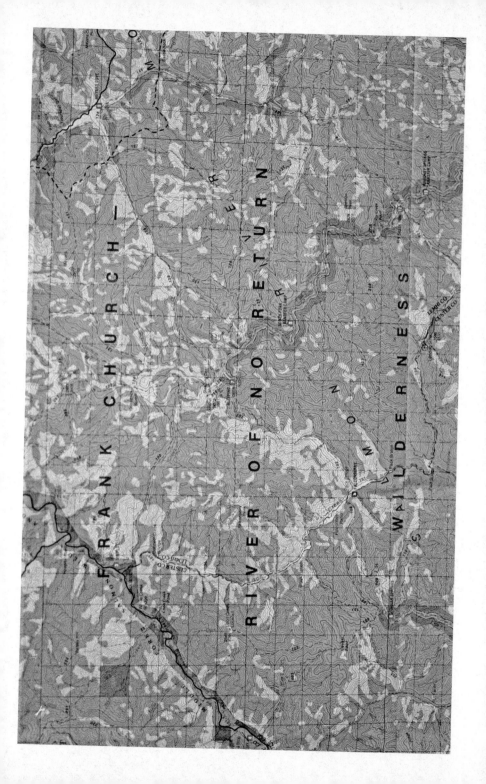

Wishful Thinking

Corey McCorkle

On The Saint-Simonians

'La Mère: She was to be *la femme libre*…This independent woman had to
be a thinking woman, one who…having fathomed the secrets of the feminine
psyche…would make confession for all her sex…The quest for…the Mother
was not an innovation of Enfantin's; well before him, Saint-Simon himself, during
the period when Augustin Thierry was his secretary, had made an attempt to
discover this…wonder...and evidently thought to have found her in Madame de
Staël. The latter declined an invitation to beget a messiah for humanity with
Saint-Simon' pp (91–93). 'The mission to locate La Mère now formed, and was
off. The pilgrims numbered 12, including Barrault, the leader of the expedition.
Their ultimate destination was Constantinople…though they had no money.
Dressed in white (as a sign of the vow of chastity they had taken on leaving
Paris), staffs in hand, they begged their way from place to place, in the name of
the Mother. In Burgundy, they hired themselves out to help with the harvest; in
Lyons, they arrived on the day before an execution and, the following morning,
demonstrated against the death penalty in front of the gallows. They embarked
in Marseilles, and worked as sailors aboard a merchant vessel whose second
mate was Garibaldi…They slept in the Great Champ des Morts, protected
by cypresses from the morning dew; they wandered throughout the bazaars,
occasionally stopping to preach the doctrines of Saint-Simon, speaking French
to Turks who could not understand them.' (pp 94–95). 'They are arrested, then
released. They set their sights on the island of Rotuma, in the South Pacific, as
the place to seek the Mother, but they get only as far as Odessa, when they are
sent back to Turkey.' According to Maxime Du Camp, *Souvenirs littéraires*, vol 3
(Paris, 1906).

The Saint-Simonian jacket buttoned in the back to emphasise brotherhood. [U17a, 2]

On the World Congress of Phalanxes.

To the Harmonians, Constantinople is the capital of the earth. [W16, 4]

Butterfly Kisses

A papillonist will retain from the outset the syllabic chronograms, such as the one which unites all the oecumenical councils in a hexameter verse.

Ni-co-e.   Ca-co-co.   Ni-co-la.   La-la-la.   Lu-lu-vi.   Flo-tri.

That is to say,

Nicomedia.	Chalendon.	Nicomedia.	Lateran.	Lugdunum.	Florence.
Constantinople.	Constantinople.	Constantinople.	Lateran.	Lugdunum.	Trident.
Epheses.	Constantinople.	Lateran.	Lateran.	Vienna.	

From 'The Papillon, or Butterfly Passion' in *The Passions Of The Human Soul And Their Influence On Society And Civilization*, Charles Fourier. [*specifically, Dactyl Hexameter*]

The Yeni Otel

Mike Nelson

The Yeni Otel

Mike Nelson

For the fourth time in my life I booked into the Yeni Otel. A man in his twenties sat behind the familiar desk, its paraphernalia of two decades still intact. Behind, hung a portrait of Atatürk – the same one, faded slightly. It still exuded an otherworldly presence that existed beyond chronological time, as opposed to a terrestrial awkwardness I had once experienced. The building had remained the same and was situated not far from the cut-through after the underwhelming train station, in a side street marked by an old Land Rover sign. The real Istanbul terminus existed over the water on the Asian side, whilst the rusting steel sign with its familiar text and font, exuded the sense of journey beginnings no longer achievable by today's backpackers. This was where the Yeni Otel, as I remembered its name, had always been.

Mehmet took me upstairs to see the room, and in a typical fit of Englishness I spoke to alleviate any awkwardness that I might pre-empt: 'I first stayed here in 1987,' I said. 'And again in '92.'

'I was born in 87,' replied Mehmet. 'August.'

'When, exactly?' I enquired with increasing curiosity.

Mehmet thought a moment to compute the date into English: 'The twentieth.'

As we looked into the twin-bedded room with the roughly cut linoleum floor that curled up the skirting board, I realised that I too had been here on that day. It was my birthdate, and I had spent that day – my twentieth birthday – in Mehmet's father's hotel as he was born.

My erratic and largely unplanned visits to Istanbul have acted like a marker in time within my adult life, and the Yeni Otel seems to hold part of me. This seemingly meaningless coincidence continues to compound that sense.

Photographs Mike Nelson
Mike Nelson is represented by 303 Gallery, New York; Galleria Franco Noero, Turin; Matt´s Gallery, London and neugerriemschneider, Berlin.

FuturePastPresent

Andreas Lang
Square Book – Cedric Price
Talking to Architects – Colin Ward

Jean Christoph Lanquetin
On The Postcolony – Achille Mbembe
A Thousand Plateaus – Gilles Deleuze and Felix Guattari
Mutations – Rem Koolhaas, Stefano Boeri, Sanford Kwinter and Nadia Tazi

Jason Coburn
The Mezzanine – Nicholson Baker
Pure War – Paul Virilio

Sovay Berriman
Consider Phlebas – Iain M Banks
A Philosophical Enquiry into the Sublime and the Beautiful – Edmund Burke

Shep Steiner
Afflicted Powers – T J Clark
The Sight of Death – T J Clark

Can Altay
The Parasite – Michel Serres
The Open – Giorgio Agamben
Swamp Thing: Earth to Earth – Alan Moore et al.

Robin Wilson
The Left Hand of Darkness – Ursula Le Guin
Utopics: The Semiological Play of Textual Spaces – Louis Marin

Sophie Warren
The Book of Sand – Jorge Luis Borges
DOMUS January 2007

Aslı Altay
The Responsibility of Form – Roland Barthes
The Man in the High Castle – Philip K Dick

Binna Choi
A Grammar of the Multitude – Paolo Virno
100 Years of Solitude – Gabriel García Márquez
Design and Crime: And Other Diatribes – Hal Foster

Library

Deniz Altay
The Secret Garden - F H Burnett

Luca Frei
Il coraggio del pettirossso – Maurizio Maggiani
Wild Thorns – Sahar Khalifeh

Jane Rendell
Yearning: Race, Gender, and Cultural Politics – bell hooks
The Literature Machine – Italo Calvino

Dirk Fleischmann
Company – Samuel Beckett
Pattern Recognition – William Gibson
No Logo – Naomi Klein

Jeremiah Day
Leaves of Hypnos – Rene Char
Somebody Blew Up America and Other Poems – Amiri Baraka

Florian Zeyfang
The Dispossessed – Ursula LeGuin
Revolution of Forms: Cuba's Forgotten Art Schools – John A Loomis

Emily Pethick
The So-Called Utopia of the Beaubourg, An Interpretation – Luca Frei
The Critical Condition – eds, Julie Ault and Martin Beck

Nav Haq
Shaping Things – Bruce Sterling

Annette Krauss
Ecology of Mind – Gregory Bateson
Essays on the Blurring of Art and Everyday Life – Allan Kaprow

Chris Fite–Wassiliak
Slaughterhouse 5 – Kurt Vonnegut
In the Fascist Bathroom – Greil Marcus

Luis Camnitzer
Fictions – Jorge Luis Borges
After Babel – George Steiner

Ethical Mop

Chris Evans

2012
46 x 21cm Component letters of an editioned wall-drawing, executed on request in blue ink with adapted marker pen by Will Holder.

E

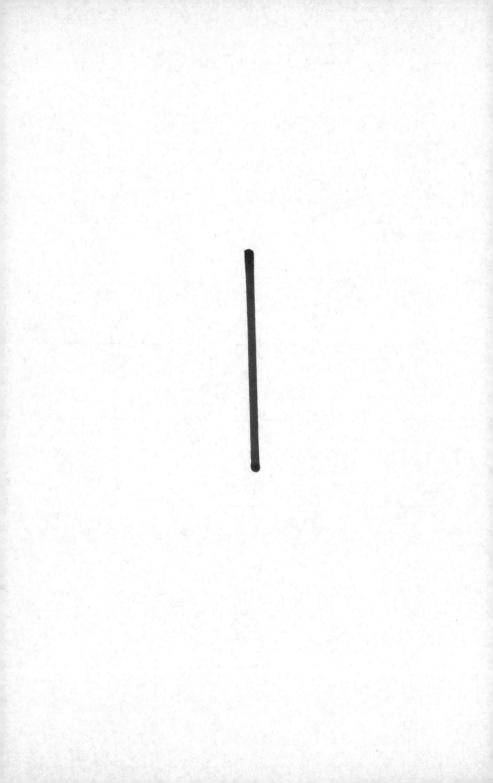

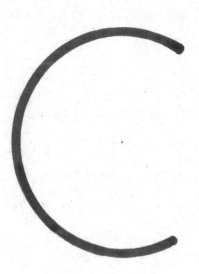

A

L

M

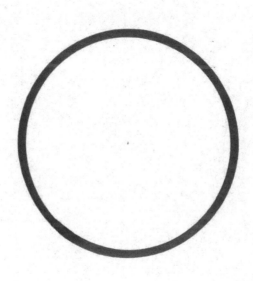

P

171

Ahali: an anthology for setting a setting
Edited by Can Altay
Published by Bedford Press
Copy editor: Sarah Handelman
Assistant editors: Çigdem Armagan, Özgür Atlagan
Design: Future Anecdotes Istanbul
Printed in Ofset Yapımevi, Sair Sokak 4, Çaglayan Mahallesi
Kagıthane, 34410, Istanbul www.ofset.com
ISBN 978-1-907414-26-8

Bedford Press
AA Publications Ltd
36 Bedford Square
London WC1B 3ES
www.bedfordpress.org

Bedford Press is an imprint of AA Publications Ltd, which
is a wholly owned subsidiary of the Architectural Assciation
(Inc) Registered Charity No 311083. Company limited by
guarantee. Registered in England No 171402. Registered
office as above.